SERGE

PRESLEY

Published by ECW PRESS
2120 Queen Street East, Suite 200, Toronto, Ontario, Canada M4E 1E2

NATIONAL LIBRARY OF CANADA CATALOGUING IN PUBLICATION DATA

Mansfield, Rex
Sergeant Presley: our untold story of Elvis' missing years / Rex and Elisabeth Mansfield
as told to Marshall and Zoe Terrill

ISBN 978-1-55022-545-7 (cloth)   ISBN 978-1-55022-555-6 (paper)

1. Presley, Elvis, 1935–1977 — Career in the military. 2. Rock musicians — United States — Biography.
I. Mansfield, Elisabeth II. Terrill, Marshall III. Terrill, Zoe IV. Title

ML420.P74M28 2002   355 .0092   C2002-902173-1

Cover and Text Design: Tania Craan
Typesetting: Wiesia Kolasinska
Production: Mary Bowness
Printing: Edwards Brothers

This book is set in Columbus and Aachen

The publication of *Sergeant Presley* has been generously supported by
the Government of Canada through the Book Publishing Industry Development Program.

Canadä

PRINTED AND BOUND IN THE UNITED STATES

ECW PRESS
ecwpress.com

SERGEANT
PRESLEY

Our Untold Story of Elvis' Missing Years

Rex and Elisabeth Mansfield
with Marshall and Zoe Terrill

ECW Press

Dedication

To Rex's mother, Bertice Roberts Mansfield, who went to be with the Lord on April 29, 1966. She lived her life before us based on the Biblical concept of Proverbs 22:6 — "Train up a child in the way he should go: and when he is old, he will not depart from it." Outside of Jesus Christ, "Mama Bertice" was the most influential person for good in our lives, as well as others, that we have ever known.

R & E

TABLE OF CONTENTS

Acknowledgments

Our thanks must first go to Elvis Presley, who created the environment that brought us together in Holy Matrimony, and also to Grandma Minnie Mae Presley, who loved Elisabeth so much that she encouraged our relationship to flourish against her own grandson. Thanks also goes to Peter and Monika Kranzler for their love and support over the years. To Jane Davis Gowen (formerly Janie Wilbanks) for helping us escape into each other's waiting arms for life. To Elisabeth's mother and sister, Ella and Linda McCormick, for loaning us saved photographs and letters to enhance our story in this book. To Ken Barker for his friendship, brotherly love, and thoughtful edit of the book. And last but not least, to Marshall and Zoe Terrill, the real authors of our book, whose probing questions and excitement about our story, continually and incessantly increased throughout the writing of this book.

Rex and Elisabeth Mansfield

Our thanks must first and foremost go to Rex and Elisabeth Mansfield, who in our opinion, have the most unique and romantic love story. These two are the classiest and warmest people we've had the pleasure to know, and it's been a privilege to tell their story. Thanks also goes to our crack editing team: Pete Ehrmann, Ken Barker, Thelma Gaba, Janet De George, Bonnie Linn, and Carolyn and Mike Terrill. Each member brought a specific gift to their editing and alternately served as a cheering section and story compass, keeping us on the straight and narrow. We'd also like to thank John Heath for his watchful eye while he factchecked our manuscript. Thanks to Roy and Chee Chee Fisher for the donation of two Elvis pictures dining at their establishment, and to Rich Consola for letting us use his letter from Elvis in 1959. And to Estelle "Gaga" Greene, for encouraging us to be dreamers, just like she is.

Marshall and Zoe Terrill

Introduction

By Rex & Elisabeth Mansfield

Elvis Presley was neither a god nor a monster, yet almost everything written about this complex and charismatic superstar portrays him as one or the other. On the one hand, Elvis was the King of Rock and Roll, rich and famous, adored by millions of fans, and one of the greatest entertainers the world has ever known — on the other hand, Elvis Aaron Presley was the son of a sharecropper, a simple country boy from Tupelo, Mississippi.

We knew Elvis at the height of his fame and popularity. When my wife Elisabeth was 19 years old, like many young women around the world, she was infatuated with his celebrity, his music, his movies, and most of all, the man himself. She couldn't have known, when she contrived a plan to get the young star's auto-graph, how that meeting would alter the course of her life forever.

Me? I was, like Elvis, a southern boy with dreams of my own, and like a lot of young American men in the years that followed World War II, I was called upon by the United States draft board to serve my country as a soldier. I knew when I was drafted in the army that my life was about to change dramatically. What I didn't know was that it wouldn't be the early mornings, the intense training, and the demanding pace of military life that would have the biggest effect on me; rather, it would be a single man, a fellow soldier, and someone who I would come to call a friend.

What follows is as much our story as it is the story of the man once known as Sergeant Elvis A. Presley, serial number U.S. 53310761. And as you will soon discover, our lives were so intertwined at the time by the forces of friendship, duty, passion, deception, and love, one story cannot be told without the other.

We will take you back in time and deep into Elvis' inner circle, each in our own words, to share with you our private memories of those years that go beyond the headlines, the fan magazines, and the books pieced together by music historians — memories of two friends in uniform and of a girl once torn between an ordinary soldier and the King of Rock and Roll.

CHAPTER ONE

Palmersville

I guess I've always been a simple country boy at heart, not unlike Elvis Presley.

I was born Donald Rex Mansfield on July 8, 1935, in the farming community of Palmersville, Tennessee — population 100. Palmersville is 120 miles north of Memphis, 120 miles west of Nashville, and is what you would call a "one-horse town."

Long known as the "red hills" area of West Tennessee, the hills are famous because of their red, clay soil. The poor soil condition makes it twice as hard to grow crops, and therefore requires much fertilizer.

Despite limited agricultural prospects, my parents, Russell and Bertice Mansfield, bought a 90-acre plot of land in 1940 for $1,200, and turned it into a successful working farm. We raised cows, pigs, and chickens, putting meat and milk on our dinner table. We grew our own vegetables, which enhanced our table even more. What we didn't consume ourselves, we sold. Growing cotton and tobacco were other profitable commodities. We even grew and baled hay to feed the cows and horses during the winter months.

Tobacco was the hardest crop to cultivate back then, because it was a 14-month process. The tobacco bed would be prepared in the fall, usually on newly cleared-off ground. This was done two months before the previous year's crop was finally sold at the tobacco auction in Murray, Kentucky.

It was back-breaking work, constantly bent over while planting, suckering, and worming (removing the tobacco worms by hand and mashing the worms heads between your thumb and forefinger). There were also the processes of removing the bottom yellow leaves, cutting down the crop when it had matured, and hanging the wilted stalks of tobacco on sticks before hauling them to the tobacco barn. Once there, the leaves were cured, stripped from the stalks, graded, tied, bundled, and prepared for the auction barn. This needed to be done by early winter so our crop, along with thousands of other tobacco farmers' crops, was readied to be sold to the highest tobacco company bidder for making cigars.

We also planted a large vegetable garden every spring, growing sweet corn, green beans, butter beans, squash, cabbage, turnip greens and turnips, tomatoes, lettuce, carrots, green and red peppers, green peas, and black-eyed peas. Sweet and Irish potatoes were also favorites. My mother canned the vegetables in Kerr jars so we could have them to eat year-round.

For a little added fun, we also grew peanuts, popcorn, grapes, cantaloupe, and watermelons. We had apple, plum, and cherry trees on the property, along with black walnut, hickory nut, and mulberry trees. Luscious, wild patches of blackberries cropped up all over the place.

Nobody would have confused us with the Rockefellers, but we always had a roof over our heads, clothes on our backs, and plenty of good food to eat. We were rich in that sense, but we didn't have anything extra. Anything we owned or acquired, we earned through the sweat of our brows.

Of course, a farm requires workers and back then you grew your own. Parents had kids to love and cherish, and also to help plow, plant and till the Back 40. My older brother Doyle and I experienced this first-hand.

It didn't take long before my father put me to work. I plowed my first row of corn at age five, which was a hilarious sight since I could barely reach the handlebars of the side-row plow. From that moment on, I haven't stopped working.

The neighboring farmers in our community would "swap work" in the fall to help get in one another's larger crops such as corn, hay, and tobacco. At 14, I could work as hard as any of the adults in our community.

When we were done learning the working aspects of the farm, I also learned to create my own fun. My cousins and I used to climb trees and pretend to be Tarzan. We would climb a 20-foot willow tree and swing down to the ground on its branches, or cut a wild grape vine at the bottom of a big tree to swing out over a pond or creek, dropping into the cool water. We also played Cowboys and Indians.

My fondest memories as a child include a horse named Belle. Belle was not only the smartest animal I ever had, but also the most affectionate. She watched out for me like a mother would her own child.

For example, I was too small to jump up on her, so she would let me take a chair, lean it against her body and crawl up onto her back. She gently and patiently waited for me until I was properly balanced. I used her mane to direct her and never needed a bridle. It was a shame I wasn't allowed to ride her to school.

Not long after plowing that first row of corn at age five, I began waking up every day at 4 a.m. to do my chores before school. They included feeding and milking the cows, feeding the horses, pigs and chickens, and gathering the eggs.

Then I had to walk one mile to meet the school bus every day because the road leading to our house was too rutted and washed out for the bus to make it to our front door. That went on for 10 years. My lucky day finally came when I was 15, as our road was finally graveled, and the bus could pick me up right in front of my house.

Palmersville School was an old-fashioned, no-nonsense public school. It was a one-story building with grades 1–12. There were 81 students in our high school when I graduated in 1954. Our senior class was the largest, with 24 students. Ninety-nine percent of them were raised on a farm.

My mother was the driving force in the family, stressing academics and hard work. I performed well in school, did my chores on the farm, and was rewarded by getting the family car on Saturday nights.

I finished high school with several academic honors, but sports were my passion, especially basketball. Our school was too small to support a football program, so "roundball" was king in Palmersville. The community rewarded us with a nice new gym. I was a first-string player on our basketball team in all four years of high school.

At 5-feet-8 inches and 140 pounds, I played point guard and was nicknamed "Little Man" by my teammates. My shortness wasn't a handicap, because I was quick and had lots of court savvy. I averaged 22 points a game during my senior year and actually led the state in scoring for a few weeks. During my senior year, we had a 26–4 record.

After I graduated from high school in 1954, my dad cut me loose from the farm.

"Well son, I got you through high school," he said. "From here on out, it's up to you on how far you want to go in life." My father was only able to get a fourth grade education before he was put to work. He wanted me to go as far as my talent would take me.

That made two of us. In fact, succeeding at all costs was my all-consuming pursuit.

The summer after graduation, I went to work at the Dresden Shoe Factory packing shoe boxes and loading them into vans for shipment. It was drudgery, but a stroll in the park compared to farm work. In fact, nothing I would ever do in life would ever be as physically hard as being raised on a red hill farm in West Tennessee.

In September 1954, after saving up enough money from the shoe factory and scoring a small scholarship, I enrolled at the University of Tennessee at Martin, about 10 miles south of Dresden.

I dated a girl named Carol Pentecost for five years. We had been going steady since the eighth grade. Carol was my first true love, and I intended to marry her one day. During the summer we continued to date exclusively, or so I thought. Then I became a little suspicious when Carol only wanted to see me on Saturday nights, claiming her studies prevented more than one date a week.

She had enrolled in summer school at UT–Martin right after our high school graduation. But higher education wasn't the only thing she was pursuing there. The truth finally came out that she was secretly dating another guy. I found out about it from a friend who lived in the same dormitory as Carol, and it just about ripped my heart out. In fact, halfway through my first quarter, I dropped out of college. I was so torn up over Carol two-timing me that I simply couldn't concentrate on my studies. I kept bumping into

Carol and her boyfriend on campus. It was such a small school that it was bound to happen. I couldn't stand it any longer so I moved to Memphis and took a job as a bank teller at Union Planters Bank.

After working six months full-time, I realized it was a dead-end job for a budding entrepreneur. Broken heart or no, I went back to UT–Martin. The tuition was expensive and I worked various jobs to make ends meet. In the morning I was a teller at the City State Bank. I waited tables during the lunch hour at the Martin Café, and took classes at the university from mid-afternoon into the evening. On weekends, I changed tires at the local Gulf service station. Somehow I managed to squeeze in time for homework and study for tests. All that sweat brought just $125 a month, barely enough to pay for room, board, and tuition.

Mr. and Mrs. Hulan Pound, owners of a dry cleaning business and daily customers at the Martin Café, admired my work ethic. In late 1956, after I had finished two years of college, they introduced me to Bob Atkinson, who offered me a full-time job driving demonstrators and selling telephone and electric utility construction equipment out of St. Louis. My starting salary was $250 per month plus travel expenses. I worked for McCabe-Powers Auto Body Company for about nine months until I was offered more money from their competitor, the Holan Corporation of Griffin, Georgia. My starting pay at the latter was $350 per month, plus one percent commission on sales, and an unlimited expense account.

I moved to Charlotte, North Carolina, and went to work for the Holan Corporation traveling and selling equipment. My territory consisted of Virginia and the Carolinas, and working it I became the success I had always dreamed of being. In 1957, I was making $10,000 a year in salary and commissions, which was a lot of money for a young, single man. Life was good. I had a nice new car, money in the bank, and I loved my job. I had nothing but a rosy future ahead of me, or so I thought until a distant relative called Uncle Sam took charge of my life.

In early March of 1958, I was on a sales call in Raleigh, North Carolina, when I decided to call my mother from my motel. We had a close relationship. Not a week went by without my calling to check on her and update her about my life. This time she was more excited than usual.

"Son, you got the most wonderful letter today from the President of the United States," mom said. "It's the nicest letter I have ever read."

President Dwight D. Eisenhower writing to me? I was really coming up in the world. Could cocktails with Kruschev be far off?

"Greetings," she started off, and right then I knew Ike didn't want to compare golf scores.

My wonderfully innocent mother didn't recognize it was a standard United States draft notice signed by the President. I was going into the Army for two years.

The Mansfield men had a history of serving their country. My brother Doyle had enlisted in the Navy during World War II. I wasn't afraid of serving my country, or unwilling to do my part, but it did come at an inconvenient time during my life. Then again, I guess there's never a convenient time to get drafted.

The next day, I called the local draft board and told them I needed some extra time to get my affairs in order. They asked me how much time I needed. I told them I would be ready on March 24, and they granted me a two-week deferral.

While I had only two weeks to prepare for the Army, another

draftee had been putting off his induction since January, 1957. That's when Elvis Presley got his first letter from the Commander-in-Chief. Elvis' manager, Colonel Tom Parker, had managed to delay Elvis' induction into the U.S. Army on account of his many career obligations. Elvis was red-hot; he was the number one entertainer in the country. In addition to his records and performing dates, he also had a few successful money-making films under his belt.

A second draft order came in April 1957, but once again, Colonel Parker had it delayed. By this time, the media were crying foul, with columnists writing that Presley was getting preferential treatment because of his celebrity status.

Not so, answered Elvis. In fact, he was anxious to switch those blue suede shoes for GI combat boots.

"Nobody has to worry about me," Presley told reporters. "I want to do my duty like every other American. My father told me, 'If you're going to be a soldier, be a good one,' and that's what I intend to do."

Elvis finally publicly announced in December 1957 that he was ready to serve his country, which caused the executives at Paramount Studios in Hollywood to just about keel over dead. Paramount had just signed Presley to a $250,000 deal to star in *King Creole*. The movie was supposed to start shooting in January, 1958, and without the world's biggest rock and roll heartthrob in the lead role they might as well not bother.

The Colonel managed to get one more deferment out of the Army until the movie *King Creole* could be finished. March 11, 1958, was Presley's last day on the set. On March 24, Elvis was ordered to report to his local draft board in his hometown of Memphis.

It was my first and Elvis' final deferment that caused our lives to intersect, and altered the course of my life forever. Call it fate, predestination, or luck of the draw but my whole life was about to change.

Early that same morning, I received a free bus ticket from my draft board in Dresden, Tennessee, and boarded the bus to Memphis with my U.S. Army draft papers in hand. I was only 22.

Arriving at the central bus station in Memphis around 11 a.m., I was surprised to find a U.S. Army staff car awaiting me, complete with a sergeant as my personal driver. At first I thought, If this is the kind of service the Army gives, I'm going to really enjoy my tour of duty! But all too soon I found out the real reason for the Army's extra special treatment.

"Soldier, how would you like to be inducted into the Army with Elvis Presley?" said the sergeant driving the staff car.

Though I wasn't much of a fan of Presley's, he was a celebrity, and frankly I was excited by the prospect of standing alongside Mr. King Creole himself when I took my Army oath. It wasn't every day a man got to be inducted with Elvis Presley, a story I could proudly tell my grandchildren one day.

"Well, of course, man. Yeah!" I said enthusiastically. "That sounds like a lot of excitement to me."

The sergeant informed me that the Army needed to gather enough new recruits for that day's induction. Regulations required a minimum number of 20 recruits so that the induction orders could be met and a military bus could be requested, departing from Memphis, Tennessee, for Fort Chaffee, Arkansas. I happened to be the very last recruit needed to fill the quota.

Experienced at repeling foreign armies in two world wars, the U.S. Army was no match against a horde of crying, screaming teenaged Elvis Presley fans. The Kennedy Veterans Memorial Hospital in Memphis was the U.S. Army induction center for all who were drafted or volunteered from West Tennessee. The Army wanted to get Elvis away from there as quickly as possible because his fans, mostly young teenaged girls, wanted desperately to catch a glimpse of "The King" and were about to crash down the hospital gates in the process.

When the sergeant and I arrived at the gates of the hospital, I got my first up-close-and-personal look at the mayhem Elvis caused wherever he went. I estimate there must have been 500 screaming, clawing, tearful fans waiting to crash the gates. It was my first taste of the excitement that surrounded this young star, and it was hard for me to understand how one man could cause that much uncontrollable excitement in so many people.

The City of Memphis Police and the Military Police proceeded slowly but surely, parting the fans to get the sergeant and me through the main gate. We then proceeded to a building where 12 other young men were waiting to be inducted that day with the King of Rock and Roll himself.

Elvis Presley was not what I had expected him to be. I saw him for the first time sitting resolutely by himself on a front row chair in the induction room, dressed in a multi-colored, checkered sport coat with stylish motorcycle-type boots. He reminded me of the Bible's description of young Joseph, all decked out in the coat of many colors which had been bestowed upon Joseph by his father Jacob.

At that moment, I sensed the same feeling Red and Sonny West and other members of the "Memphis Mafia" later expressed when they came into contact with Elvis: I immediately wanted to protect him, for reasons I could not begin to understand.

As strange as that may be to say about someone you have never met, it's how I felt. Everything Elvis Presley did was in front of an audience watching his every move. He was a lonely-looking young man that day. Somewhere deep inside of myself, I instinctively knew we were going to become close friends. Call it intuition, call it discernment. Whatever it was, I just felt it from the pit of my stomach.

Normally at an induction, a military recruit is usually given a thorough four-hour medical examination. Nothing was normal about that one. My physical was a "condensed" version that took all of five minutes.

"You look pretty healthy, kid. You pass," was basically how it went. The point was to get the induction process over quickly so Elvis could move on. Ten minutes later, I was standing with Elvis and a roomful of strangers, holding my right hand up and being sworn into the United States Army.

"I, Rex Mansfield, do solemnly swear that I will have true faith and allegiance to the United States of America. That I will serve them honestly and faithfully against all enemies whomsoever and I will obey the orders of the United States and all the officers appointed over me, according to all regulations in the uniform code of the military service." With that, I was officially a member of the United States Army.

Besides Elvis and myself, the other men inducted that day were Timothy Christopher, Jr., Gilmore Daniel, Farley R. Guy, Louis G. Hern, Wallace J. Hoover, Robert T. Maharrey, Alex E. Moore, William C. Montague, William R. Norvell, James Payne, Jr., Nathaniel Wigginson, Tommy A. Dabbs, Wayne D. Morton, William K. Sandlin, Kenneth C. Reynolds, Franklin D. Lax, James E. Vaughn, and Jerry E. Morris.

As soon as the oath was administered, all of us boarded an awaiting olive drab Army bus parked just outside the front door of the induction building. Before we boarded, I looked outside the window and noticed Colonel Tom Parker deeply entrenched in conversation with Elvis. It appeared as if he were giving Elvis special instructions of what was going to go down that day.

On the bus, every man took a double seat for himself since there were only 20 of us. Elvis was the last man to get on, and the first to break the silence. As we pulled away from the induction station, Elvis' father, Vernon Presley, was backing up his brand new black Cadillac limousine. Vernon was trying to turn it around so he and his wife, Gladys, could watch us leave and wave goodbye to their son.

As they waved farewell to their son from each side of the Cadillac's opened front door windows and our bus was driving away, Elvis finally spoke.

"Well, goodbye you long, black sonofabitch!" he said, half-sad, half-joking.

The remark drew smiles and chuckles from his fellow grunts.

Elvis was "officially" one of the boys.

CHAPTER TWO

Fort Chaffee, Arkansas
— Being Processed

When Elvis Presley stepped on that bus, he was Private E-1 Elvis A. Presley, SERIAL NUMBER U.S. 53310761, now property of the United States, a Government Issue commonly known as a "GI."

"Heaven knows I want to live up to what people expect of me," Elvis had said to a reporter. It was a time in history when you did what your government told you to do. But the Army knew that #53310761 was no regular buck private, and acted accordingly.

I'll never forget the sight of all those young girls violently pulling and shoving each other just to get one more glimpse of Elvis. Some were even hanging off the bus as the Army took their idol away from them and civilian life.

While the chaos outside the hospital didn't appear to rattle Elvis whatsoever, it was something foreign to us regular folk. We were all wondering how this guy could be so casual about all those girls who wanted a piece of him. All he did was smile and blow kisses to them.

The girls put up a valiant fight, but the bus slowly pulled out of their grasp, and a few of them chased us until it became hopeless. We got through the gate and headed down through Memphis.

As we made our way to West Memphis crossing the Mississippi River bridge into Arkansas, I noticed we weren't alone. An endless caravan of automobiles followed the Army bus. We were provided a military and civilian police escort all the way across the bridge. After we crossed the river and headed out into the countryside of Arkansas on Highway 70, we noticed that the caravan of cars finally began to dwindle down to a few hardcore fans. But rein-forcements were on the way.

We made a stop in West Memphis at Earl's Hot Biscuits for coffee. No one was supposed to know we were scheduled to stop at that particular roadside restaurant, but that didn't stop 200 Elvis Presley fans from meeting us there.

The bus driver and most of the guys got off the bus and feasted on sandwiches and soft drinks, while poor Elvis was forced to eat on the bus. The traveling fan club's presence was actually no accident or coincidence, as the sight of Colonel Tom Parker handing out signed 8 x 10's of his boy indicated.

Colonel Tom Parker was an intersesting character to say the least. I later discovered he successfully rose from the carnival ranks to manage country acts such as Eddy Arnold and Hank Snow, and took them to the top of their profession. When Elvis arrived on the scene in the mid-1950s, Parker was in the right place at the right time when he took over as Presley's manager in 1955. Pear-shaped and rotund, Parker was not physically imposing, but anyone could tell when he was in Elvis' presence, he was the one calling the shots. Though the Army might have been Elvis' boss for the next two years, the Colonel was still able to pull rank with Uncle Sam as far as his boy was concerned.

While I had no direct contact with the Colonel, I watched him

16

from afar with amusement and admiration, looking to squeeze everthing form the media on behalf of his client. Looking back, I must say he did an excellent job.

In 1956, Elvis Presley dominated the musical landscape when he released a string of several million-selling singles. They included: "Heartbreak Hotel," "Don't Be Cruel," "Hound Dog," "I Want You, I Need You, I Love You," "Blue Suede Shoes," and "Love Me Tender."

A stream of Elvis products — lipsticks, towels, pajamas, perfumes — bombarded the market and sold with startling ease. America couldn't get enough of Elvis Presley. Naturally, Hollywood came calling.

In April, 1956, Elvis signed a seven-picture deal with Paramount Pictures for $100,000 a picture, making him a movie star as well.

At the same time, Parker was promoting him like a bar of soap. The Colonel guarded against Elvis' overexposure by carefully regulating his appearances on national television. If you wanted contact with Elvis, you went through the Colonel.

The talent and charisma belonged to Elvis — but make no mistake — the Colonel ran the show.

That didn't stop once Elvis joined the Army, but as that first pit stop en route to Fort Chaffee showed, now he had to do it behind the scenes.

After we got back on Highway 70, we drove for another 90 miles. We stopped next in North Little Rock at a family owned place called Roy Fisher's Steak House on 1919 E. Broadway — a place that is still open today for business.

While the rest of the soldiers went in through the front of the restaurant, Elvis was escorted through the back door and met up with us in a private dining room. The food was all homemade and tasty as could be, as it still is today. The best part was, the whole spread was on Uncle Sam.

After we finished our meal, we got back on the bus and made the last leg of the drive, which was another 115 miles. We arrived in Fort Chaffee about 11:15 p.m. Amazingly, there were still a few cars filled with loyal, hardcore fans that tailed us right to the gate.

Of course, Elvis was obviously accustomed to such madness. The rest of us were amazed by the whole affair, but we also loved every minute of it. We all felt as if we were a part of Elvis as we shared some of his limelight.

I couldn't help but feel sorry for the fans turned away from the Fort Chaffee Military Base. It was a long ride back to Memphis. Not for Colonel Parker though — he and the media had clearance to follow us into the base.

All of us were exhausted by the fanfare of our first day in the Army. Upon arriving at camp, poor Elvis still had to pose for pictures and conduct interviews in a special reception room. The rest of us gladly hit the sack and were instantly asleep once our quarters were sorted out. Although the Army generally tolerated the media frenzy, the line was drawn when a photographer was found hiding in the barracks. He wanted to take a candid picture of Elvis sleeping in his quarters. The way that guy flew out of there, he should have tried the Air Force. For most of us, traveling with Elvis had been the most exciting event of our lives. I was quick to learn that this first day of insane excitement was only the beginning of many more to follow. The best was yet to come.

Magazine and newspaper reporters were only allowed to follow Elvis at certain times, and always under the Colonel's supervision. The Army did a fantastic job of protecting Elvis, and added extra Military Police to escort us. Their security was excellent.

The next day, Elvis was already dressed and shaved by the time the rest of us even woke up. The Colonel and many of the photographers joined him for breakfast for more pictures. Even though it wasn't the kind of food Elvis was accustomed to, he was hungry and said that everything tasted good.

At the Fort Chaffee dispensary, the new inductees received several inoculations and were handed our first military paycheck. It totaled $7 for the day. A reporter asked Elvis what he was going to do with all that money.

"Start a loan company," Elvis answered with a ready smile.

We all were issued our allotments of olive drab uniforms (OD's), fatigues, boots, socks, underwear, rain gear, shelter halves, and a duffel bag in which to carry it all. After we were assigned our new apparel, we practiced folding and fitting it all into the duffel bag. It sounds like Beetle Bailey stuff, but actually it was a skill that required serious precision and execution.

We then received our matching GI haircuts. When Elvis got his, Colonel Parker was present and accounted for. He had arranged for several photographers and camera crews to document his boy's precious locks getting sheared.

"Hair today, gone tomorrow," Elvis quipped to over 50 photographers and newsmen as he was given his regulation Army buzz-cut. At least he had a sense of humor about the whole thing. Then he forgot to pay the sixty-five cent fee to the barber, and had to be summoned back for payment.

We spent the remainder of our time in Fort Chaffee under Sergeant Francis Johnson taking written and oral tests. These tests were designed to help the Army determine what each new recruit was best qualified to do, or so we were told. Elvis and the rest of us had a big laugh because of what happened following completion of the tests.

Guys who were class-A auto mechanics in civilian life were made cooks, guys who were highly qualified chefs in civilian life were made mechanics, truck drivers became office clerks while office clerks became truck drivers, and so forth. It seemed the Army was bound and determined to place each one of us into something completely opposite of that for which our civilian training qualified us.

In fact, the Army had already decided our fate before the tests were even given.

After the testing and indoctrination, seven of the original 13 Memphis inductees were loaded on buses and sent to various military training bases around the country.

Six of us — including Alex Moore, Nathaniel Wigginson, Wallace Hoover, William Norvell, and Elvis and me — were loaded into another military bus with other new recruits and sent to Fort Hood, Texas. Fort Hood was located about 150 miles south of the Dallas-Fort Worth Metroplex; approximately 15 miles west of Temple, and very near to a little town called Killeen.

At that time, Fort Hood was the largest military base in the United States, with about 50,000 troops stationed there mostly for the purpose of basic and advanced basic training of soldiers.

We had barely slept during the four days of in-processing procedures at Fort Chaffee. But we got no sympathy from the Army as our butts were rolled out of bed at 3 a.m., and we were ordered to pack our duffel bags and be ready to leave for Fort Hood in an hour. It would be one long day as we traveled about 500 miles south through Oklahoma to "Deep in the Heart of Texas."

As I would soon discover, when Uncle Sam told us to jump, we asked, "How high?"

CHAPTER THREE

Fort Hood, Texas
— Basic Training

The Memphis fans turned back at Fort Chaffee were replaced with new fans from Arkansas, who planned to follow us into Texas. It was unreal.

Originally we were slated to stop for lunch in Waxahachie, a few miles south of Dallas. The Colonel (Parker that is) had leaked it again that we would be stopping at a restaurant in Waxahachie, but the Army was now in charge of Elvis.

To avoid the 400 fans that awaited Elvis, it was decided that we would keep going and try to find some out of the way place where Elvis could get off the bus and enjoy a peaceful lunch with the rest of us. Nobody protested (as if it would've made a difference), and on we went. But, by about 1:30 p.m. everyone was famished. We took a detour off the main highway into a town called Hillsboro, located about halfway between Dallas and Waco.

Along the way, somehow the bus driver had managed to elude the reporters and fans that were following us. There was no crowd waiting for us at the diner where we stopped. For about 25 minutes we enjoyed the peace and quiet of a normal lunch, but then things changed abruptly. The reporters and fans that had been following us, along with the ones who were already waiting at the Waxahachie stop, finally figured out where we were. When they converged at the diner, a small riot ensued. Already upset about being stood up in Waxahachie, now the fans were determined to get Elvis no matter what.

The rest of us GI's took our cue from Elvis, who was obviously accustomed to such madness. We surrounded him, and pushed and shoved irate reporters and fans aside as we made our way back on the bus. The local police were called in to calm the situation and help us get out of town and back on the road. By the time the cars surrounding our bus were ordered to move, and the fans cleared out of our path, it was almost an hour later before we made our way out of town.

Elvis was the second GI off the bus when we arrived about two hours later at Fort Hood. The media surrounded him and showered him with questions. They even requested that he salute. He was good-natured and obliged. Elvis strained to answer reporters' intrusive questions, several of which bordered on being rude. Army spokesperson Lieutenant Colonel Marjorie Schulten finally stepped in and stated this would be Elvis' final press conference. According to Schulten, Elvis was "just another soldier." I suppose she would've called the 40-day flood "just another rainstorm."

As Elvis ate his first Army meal at Fort Hood, which consisted of fish and French fries, a group of girls rallied outside the mess hall.

"Let us see him and we'll go away!" they cried out. A good number of these girls were dependent children of the training corps stationed at Fort Hood. The Military Police were called to disband them. From that point on during our basic training, the girls as well as the press were barred from our training areas on the base.

That left the telephone, and Fort Hood was inundated by calls for Private Presley. Elvis could make outgoing phone calls like the rest of us, but he could not receive calls unless it was a family emergency. The Army set up a system to screen all the calls for Elvis and simply told the callers he was not allowed to receive any phone calls. Actually, this was not so different from the rules we had to follow, except the volume of calls for Elvis was a real headache for the Fort Hood telephone operators.

Fort Hood was first referred to as Camp Hood, and stood as the biggest Army post in the United States. The 335-square mile installation was designed in 1942 out of ranch and farmland to closely resemble the region in Germany where GI's received advanced training. It was set up this way so American soldiers could acclimate themselves to Europe-like conditions.

We had been told in a sort of joking, tongue-in-cheek manner, that our tests had determined we would make good tankers. We were assigned to various companies, platoons, and squads, comprising the 2nd Armored Division. It was the World War II tank division called "Hell on Wheels," made famous by General George Patton.

Our full training program did not begin until approximately four weeks later. The reason for the delayed training was that our company was waiting until all the recruits arrived and we were up to our full strength of 220 men.

A basic training company of recruits consists of four platoons with 55 men in each platoon. A platoon consists of five squads of 10 men, plus five squad leaders. There would be a total of 28 training companies (or over 6,000) men taking basic training at the same time. It took some time to get that many people drafted and processed from all over the United States. They had to be transported across country and assigned to their training company. Even though the full training was delayed, we were still required to be out of bed every morning just before five o'clock.

A typical day before basic training started included getting up and making up our bunk beds, falling out (running outside and lining up in our squads and platoon), and roll call (when your name was called, you had to call out, "Here Sir!"). The purpose of roll call was to make sure no one had gone Absent Without Leave (AWOL). Immediately after roll call came the daily dozen exercises consisting of 12 exercises done 12 times each.

We took off our fatigue shirts and performed these exercises while dressed in OD T-shirts, fatigue pants and combat boots. Each platoon exercised in unison under the direction of its platoon sergeant. If we got out of synch too often, the sarge made us fall down and crank out 100 push-ups.

After the daily dozen, which took one hour, we went back to our barracks, took a shower, put on clean OD underwear, fatigues, socks, cap, and polished combat boots, cleaned our barracks, (including the latrines), then got in the chow line for breakfast at 6:30 a.m.

After breakfast we policed the area, mostly picking up cigarette butts. If a recruit missed or walked over a butt without picking it up, he would have to do 100 pushups. When our area was cleaned, we fell in for training in the fine art of marching, which consisted of, well, marching around for 55 minutes without stopping. After a five-minute break, we would march another hour with another five-minute break. This went on every morning until noon chow.

The afternoons and evenings varied, but included routines such as washing the barrack floors with soap and water, cleaning windows, spit-shining our boots, cleaning our mess gear, kitchen patrol (KP), guard duty, orientation (classroom work), learning the nomenclature of all our gear, and, at long last, standing in the chow line for dinner.

After dinner, which ended our workday around 7 p.m., we had free time. Most of us were so tired from the day's activities that all we wanted to do was hit the sack. Some guys might play cards or write home, but the lights went out promptly at 9 p.m. followed by a bed roll call.

By the time our real basic training started in four weeks, we were already in such a training mode that the difference was hardly noticeable. The major difference was that we were issued weapons, an M-1 rifle, which we had to take apart, clean and reassemble every day.

Our marching then changed to close order drill, and our platoon sergeant became a tough drill sergeant. With rifles on our shoulders we had to learn to perform all kinds of close order maneuvers without knocking each other's heads off with our rifle barrels.

After our early morning daily dozen and a full morning of close order drills, followed by a big lunch at the mess hall, the hardest thing was to stay awake during the afternoon classroom work. We were studying details in army manuals covering our training. Next to that, reading the phone book was positively racy. While they were undoubtedly well informed, some of our instructors, with their monotone delivery and totally humorless personalities, made it as interesting as watching grass grow.

The 2nd Armored Division had recently rotated from Germany to Fort Hood to become the tank training division for all tankers, replacing the 3rd Armored Division which was being sent to Germany.

When the Army rotated these divisions, the 50-ton tanks, six-wheel drive army trucks, jeeps, and all other equipment were rotated at the same time. If anyone can tell me why the United States Government would allow the Army to do that, that person's smarter than me. The cost must have been enormous. It would have made more sense to keep the military equipment in the same place and transfer only the men.

We took all of our training under the 2nd Armored Division, which was known as one of the best divisions in the Army and was also known to be tough as hell, which is why it was named "Hell on Wheels."

Elvis stayed in the barracks with the rest of his platoon. The two of us, along with 218 other men, were assigned to Company A, 2nd Medium Tank Battalion, 37th Armor, 2nd Armored Division for basic training. Every arriving recruit was given $20 in cash for additional haircuts and toiletries, including Elvis.

"Presley, give me that $20; you don't need it!" one of the sergeants ordered.

"Sergeant, I'm broke!" Elvis shrugged.

Elvis really tried hard to be just one of the boys. He participated in every training class, every field trip, and marched alongside us for hours.

Most of us usually watched him from the corners of our eyes. We were very skeptical and expected Elvis to ask for and receive extra attention and favors. But I can honestly say that from the very start, Elvis never asked for special treatment. He went through basic training just like the rest of us. Actually, it was even harder on him because Elvis was constantly under scrutiny from prying eyes. The pressure on him must have been enormous, but he never complained. The rest of us were constantly whining about everything, which is normal for a bunch of GI's. If GI's are not bitching, something is wrong.

Elvis' musical talent even came in handy. He played the drums for us when we marched. It was standard practice to pick one guy that could play drums, and Elvis happened to be the only guy in our platoon who knew how to play and keep time.

I saw a lot of guys during those first few weeks try to push themselves on Elvis. It was downright sickening what some people would do in an attempt to get close to him. But Elvis was very intuitive. He was wary of people who tried to push themselves on him, and they never got to first base. I witnessed grown men fawn all over him, throw their arm around him pretending he was their pal, even asking for autographs or photos with Elvis. The most embarrassing moments were when I saw GI's racing to stand next to him in the chow line. It was obvious that Elvis had a lot of experience with people like that. He could distinguish who was sincere and who wanted a quick brush with fame, or maybe even a handout.

I will freely admit that I wanted to be a friend to Elvis myself. Heck, who wouldn't like to have a celebrity as a personal friend? But I knew a little about people and I realized if I tried to push myself on Elvis, I'd never be his friend. For the previous two years I had been making my living traveling through 13 southeastern states as a salesman. Any decent salesman has to know how people act and react to given situations. If he wants to sell his product, he must first sell himself. So, I decided to cool it with Elvis and wait for the right time. I figured if we were meant to be friends, it would happen easy and naturally. I cannot explain why, but I knew deep down something would eventually happen to bring us together.

The first Army buddy of Elvis' was a guy named William Norvell. Elvis nicknamed him "Nervous Norvell" because he had a high-pitched voice, was overprotective of Elvis and generally seemed nervous about everything. The nickname seemed to suit him well.

Norvell and Elvis were in the same platoon and barracks. I was assigned to the platoon and barracks next door to theirs. Elvis, Norvell and I were made squad leaders at the start of the basic training. We wore these arm bands which had two stripes, and we were called Acting Squad Leaders (among other things). We were given the jobs due to our past military experience — Norvell and I had previously been in the National Guard, and Elvis had been in Reserve Officers Training Corps (ROTC) at Humes High School. Just about anyone with even a little prior military experience was made a squad leader.

We liked being squad leaders because we never had to pull KP (kitchen patrol) and we never had to walk during our guard duty. When our names were put on the guard duty roster, we were always Corporal of the Guard. This meant we placed the walking guards on and off their assigned post every two hours. We had to stay up almost all night checking on the guards to make sure their duties were being properly performed. If any of the walking guards goofed off, the Corporal of the Guard always caught hell. Otherwise, being a squad leader in basic training was not really being favored, as we had more responsibility and less time off than the regular recruits.

Our training was going well, although it was hot as blazes. The temperature in Killeen, in mid-summer could reach a scorching 110 degrees in the shade. During one 15-mile march, about half the company passed out from heat exhaustion. It sure melted off the surplus weight, and we started to get into excellent physical condition.

After about four weeks of basic training, we were able to get weekend passes, providing we weren't on some kind of duty roster like guard duty. It was a Friday night, early in the evening around 8 o'clock, and Anita Wood had made the 600-mile trek from Memphis to be with Elvis.

Anita was a former beauty queen from Jackson, Tennessee, and also a co-host of Wink Martindale's Memphis TV show, *Top Ten Dance Party*, a Saturday program for teenagers. In July 1957, she and Elvis started seeing each other regularly, and at this time in Elvis' life, she was his number one girl. To me she was the typical all-American southern belle with a wonderful sense of humor. Everybody liked Anita, and it was obvious why Elvis liked her.

When she arrived, Elvis was scheduled for guard duty for the next 24 hours. What happened next was quite normal. A GI in basic training on guard duty could have someone of equal rank pull his guard for him, providing the Sergeant of the Guard approved the substitution.

With the permission of Sergeant Bill Norwood, our company's top kick, Elvis came to me with his dilemma. I was sitting on my bunk in my barracks when Elvis approached. With a genuine show of humility, he asked if I would mind pulling his guard duty. He explained that the switch was already approved by Norwood, and offered me a large numbered bill to take his place. There were probably hundreds of other guys who would have jumped at the chance to pull his guard duty, but Elvis picked me. I told him straight away that I would be glad to help him out, but that he didn't have to bother forking over any dough.

"Elvis, I would do this for any other GI whose girl was waiting to see him," I told him. I wasn't lying or laying it on thick. I would've done it for anybody else, and I wanted Elvis to know it.

Elvis liked the way I had handled myself in this matter, and that marked the real beginning of our friendship. Maybe he was testing me, I really don't know. However, from that day forward, Elvis and I began to develop a closer relationship.

Slowly and cautiously, but surely, Elvis included me in his world. I could really feel that he sincerely wanted me to be one of his close friends. Often we would be on guard duty at the same time. We enjoyed trading stories, comparing our platoon sergeants, talking about which instructors were really good, and who was downright boring, and which guys in our platoons and squads were goof-offs, and which were gung-ho.

I don't recall during which guard duty Elvis walked up to me and laid his arm on my shoulder and said, "Rex, what do you think of —" whatever subject was on his mind. But this became a routine between us, and it made me feel I was someone important to him, and that he valued me as a friend. Still, I remained very careful not to push myself on him too much.

We had many good talks on a variety of subjects during the remainder of our basic training. Cars were a subject we enjoyed. Elvis told me about all the different cars he owned, and we'd discuss the latest models with the most powerful engines. We would talk about how we were raised, the things we liked and didn't like to eat; and, of course, we talked about the ladies. Elvis told me about the Hollywood starlets he had met and what it was like to make a movie. I found out he was a very down-to-earth guy who needed sincere friends in order to stay sane.

In time, Elvis bestowed a nickname on me. He called me,

"Rexadus." There was no particular reason for this name, I think he just liked it. It was fine by me.

Anita Wood stayed at Fort Hood a few weeks, and Elvis would see her quite often. Since Anita was staying with Sergeant and Mrs. Bill Norwood, who lived in government housing on the post, Elvis could slip over and see Anita during the week when he was off-duty. He didn't get into trouble since Sergeant Norwood knew where he was at all times, and it didn't impinge on his assigned duties. While Elvis was on duty as a soldier, he never received special treatment. However, when he was off duty, he got some minor concessions such as Norwood opening his home to him.

Norwood sensed right from the beginning how homesick Elvis was. He needed someone to look out for him, and the Sergeant was the right one to do that. Elvis would call his mother from Norwood's home so they could converse in private.

"When you come into my house, you can let it all out," Norwood said.

On some weekends, Elvis would take Anita up to Waco, Texas, to stay with Eddie and Lanelle Fadal. Elvis had met Eddie in 1956, when he played at the Heart of Texas Coliseum in Waco. Norvell and his wife went with them once or twice, but Elvis never asked me to go until our second stage of training, called advanced basic.

Elvis asked Norvell to bring his wife to stay with Anita during the day. Somewhere close to the end of basic training, Anita and Mrs. Norvell were sent home so we could immerse ourselves in training.

Training was much too demanding to have anything physically or emotionally left over to give to anyone at the end of the day. It would have been an insult to have asked the girls to hang around. The additional training included a confidence course that covered an area about the size of a football field, and was practically solid with jagged, sharp-edged rocks ranging in size from eggs to grapefruits. Furthermore, the course was covered with thousands of barbed wire strands positioned just high enough for a man to crawl under on his back or belly. If one was very cautious, he would not get hung up but every 10 feet or so. Big coils of barbed wire were inlaid all through the course underneath the top strands.

As part of our training, we had to crawl on our backs through the course while live 30- and 50-caliber machine gun fire was being directed about two feet from our heads. Then we had to do the whole course again on our bellies, holding the M-1 rifle between our arms. When we finished the belly crawl, our knees and elbows were skinned bloody. But there was no rest, because the same night we had to go through the whole thing again in the dark. At night, the machine guns fired tracer ammunition and we could actually see the bullets pass over our heads. It was a pretty scary ordeal.

The Army has a secret formula in its basic training program. If a guy goes in overweight, he will come out slim; if he goes in too slim, he will gain weight. The funny part about this is everybody gets the same training and the same food. I weighed 190 pounds when I was inducted. At the end of basic, I had trimmed down to a svelte 150 pounds. Elvis was neither fat nor thin, so training only served to make him tougher, and both of us could have run into a solid brick wall at full speed and just bounced off. We were in top form and at the peak of our physical abilities.

When basic was finished, everyone received a 14-day, well-deserved leave. I knew I was really getting close to Elvis when he asked me, along with Norvell, to ride back to Memphis with him in his new white Lincoln Continental Mark IV. We didn't need any time to think it over, and on May 31 we started the long road trip back to Memphis. I was being given a personal escort by Elvis Presley, and he was going to show me his home, called Graceland.

CHAPTER FOUR

Graceland or Bust

On our drive back to Memphis in Elvis' beautiful Mark IV Lincoln Continental, I learned a great deal about Elvis the man as we reflected on the past eight weeks of U.S. Army basic training.

We had been put through one of the toughest and most physically demanding training programs offered by the U.S. Army. Elvis appeared to enjoy the entire program and made every effort to be a good soldier. He had gained everyone's respect at Fort Hood through his hard work and determination.

We reminisced about how initially the guys teased Elvis, saying such things as, "Where's yore hound dawg?" and, "Ain't y'all lonesome tonight without yore teddy bear?" We laughed about the sweet revenge exacted on a regular tormenter outside of our outfit who would harass Elvis while we were marching in formation to our next duty. Sergeant Norwood called out, "COMPANY HALT," then walked right up to the perpetrator, got right in his face, and slowly chewed him out, up one side and down the other.

Army regulations gave Sergeant Norwood the authority to reprimand a soldier based on the military code that forbade soldiers from talking to individuals in a marching formation. Sometimes he would humiliate the transgressors further by making them fall down right in front of everyone and do 50 push-ups.

That sort of thing became unnecessary toward the end of basic training, as Elvis received more accolades, especially when he won a Marksman medal with a rifle and a Sharpshooter medal with a pistol.

As we drove in the direction of Memphis, we also discussed surviving the confidence course, and the culmination of our basic training, which was a 15-mile march to bivouac with a 70-pound field pack on our backs. During the week of bivouac, we trained all day in the field and slept in tents at night with the rattlesnakes.

"Bivouac" was the name for living in tents and training in the field in combat-like conditions. Our favorite memory of bivouac was when a training sergeant lassoed a big king snake and led it toward a group of us as we sat in a circle. Another sergeant, who was giving us instruction at the time, must have stared death in the face many times in combat, but none of that rattled him as much as the sight of that snake. He took off running like a wild horse, not to be seen again that day.

We were taught how to fire the M-1 Rifle along with other infantry weapons, and how to use the bayonet in hand-to-hand combat. We were issued gas masks and then sent into a building filled with tear gas and ordered to remove them, hold our breath, and slowly walk outside without panicking. We had to open our eyes to see how to get out of the shelter, and man, our eyes burned and teared like a Glenn Miller fan seeing Elvis Presley for the first time.

The training was very rigid and grueling, and Elvis went through it just like the rest of us. No complaints. We were proud to be partnered with such a stalwart soldier.

As we inched closer to Memphis, Elvis began to reminisce about his childhood.

Born January 8, 1935, into poverty in Tupelo, Mississippi, Elvis and his mother shared a special bond because of the death of his twin brother, Jesse Garon, a stillborn. Gladys Presley was never able to have another child and desperately clung to her only son.

The Presley family was very much involved with the church, which sparked Elvis' passion for music.

When Elvis was three, his father, Vernon, went to the Mississippi State Penitentiary for altering a $4 check. Gladys and son moved in with relatives next door until Vernon was released. Elvis spent much of his time with his relatives during the week. On weekends, Gladys and Elvis traveled by bus, a 10-hour round trip, to visit Vernon. Gladys grew even more protective of Elvis, fearing she would lose her entire family.

Upon his release, Vernon had no real job prospects and moved wherever he could to find work. Gladys took refuge from their desperate poverty by showering Elvis with all of her attention. She never took her eyes off him when he played outside, and walked him to school every day. Elvis was an average student and somewhat reserved.

On Elvis' eleventh birthday, his parents bought him his first guitar. At this point in his young life, he had already proved in church and in a talent show that he was blessed with the ability to sing. Elvis had wanted a bicycle, but Gladys revealed the cost was too much and feared he might get injured. She and Vernon settled on the guitar. Elvis' Uncle Vester, who enjoyed country music, showed him how to strum a few chords.

Elvis became more and more engrossed in music and really applied himself. He familiarized himself with the instrument. He put on shows and delighted in singing and entertaining, inspired by all types of music from many different ethnic backgrounds.

This is what ultimately made his sound and style unique.

Eventually, the Presley family moved to Memphis in search of a better life. But times remained lean for the family, as they struggled to make it financially. During high school, Elvis remained a shy and reserved mama's boy, but his music helped him find solace as well as form friendships.

Shortly after Elvis turned 16, he joined Humes High School's ROTC program, which was a good experience for his future stint in the Army. Throughout high school, Elvis worked odd jobs to help support his family and still made time to frequent "all-night" gospel sings at the Memphis Auditorium.

After graduating in June of 1953, Elvis continued to work a string of jobs while pursuing his dreams of recording music. On a Saturday morning in July, Elvis dropped by Sun Records. He paid a small fee and recorded two songs titled "My Happiness" and "That's When Your Heartaches Begin." It was just his majestic voice and his sweet guitar. Elvis claimed the record was a surprise for his mother. The rest, as they say, is history.

As we drove on, Elvis began discussing the highs and lows of show business. He revealed how much he missed his career and how he longed to make more records and movies, expressing genuine concern that two years away from the limelight might hurt his career, and disclosed that several songs had been pre-recorded for periodic release during his military service to prevent that from happening.

He even got into his 20-year contract with RCA and several movie contracts the Colonel had lined up for him when he returned from overseas duty. He also had designs on performing in Las Vegas when the price Colonel Parker demanded was met. The Colonel was holding out for $50,000 a week, an amount that doesn't sound like much by today's astronomical standards, but back in the 1950s was unheard of. (Incidentally, Elvis waited until 1969 for Las Vegas to finally meet the Colonel's price.)

The Mark IV included a car phone, another rarity in 1958. As we approached West Memphis, Arkansas, he handed the phone to Norvell to call his wife and arrange to meet her at a certain place. When we arrived at the designated stop in Memphis, she was there waiting. Elvis then allowed me to call my brother, Doyle. I had already arranged for my family to drive down to Memphis from Dresden to pick me up. They were at the home of Quinton Olds, distant relatives by marriage, in North Memphis.

Elvis had me tell Doyle that I would be driven over to meet him in about an hour. Elvis wanted me to spend a little more time with him, to meet his parents and friends and show me around Graceland.

That was the beauty of Elvis' friendship; he was very giving of himself. He made you a part of what he was. It was a feeling of honor and prestige to be treated this way by Elvis. If he liked you and considered you a friend, there wasn't anything in the world he wouldn't do for you.

Elvis was on the car phone quite a bit himself, talking to his mother and father. He also spoke to several of his old civilian buddies. They were all waiting anxiously for his arrival. It was going to be a great homecoming for Elvis, and incredibly, I was going to be a part of it.

As we passed through the musically designed wrought iron gates and drove up the winding circular driveway, for the first time in my life, I laid eyes on the splendid and beautiful Graceland Mansion.

Graceland is known to millions today as the home of Elvis Presley, but originally it was named after the 500 acres that surrounded the home. In 1861, it was established as a Hereford cattle farm by S.E. Toof, the publisher of the *Memphis Commercial Appeal*. He named it "Graceland" in honor of his daughter, Grace Toof. It was Ruth Moore, Grace's niece, who built the house in 1939.

Elvis made an offer of $100,000 to Ruth Moore, who was separated from her husband at the time. That was March 19, 1957. Elvis purchased the mansion mainly for his mother, Gladys, but also as a sanctuary for himself as his popularity continued to snowball.

On April 10th, the Presley family moved in. Mrs. Presley, a highly religious woman, said many times that it was only through the grace of God were they able to live in such a beautiful mansion.

It was located on top of a hill in the back center of about 10 acres of beautifully landscaped property with lots of trees. The entire property was surrounded by an eight-foot brick wall.

As we made our way past the gates, about a hundred or so fans were screaming for Elvis' attention. We did not stop for Elvis to dispense his usual autographs because he was very tired and anxious to get inside. I remember when we drove past the fans, the full-time gatekeepers promised them that Elvis would come back later and sign autographs.

The treatment I received from Elvis upon our arrival at the front of his mansion was truly amazing to me. After a round of hugs and kisses for his parents, and warm greetings to his friends, he turned all his attention to me.

Elvis' mother and father were thrilled that I had come home with their beloved son. They were extremely pleasant and very much appreciated me as one of Elvis' close Army buddies. It was easy to see how proud they were of Elvis. His parents seemed to love and admire their son almost to the point of worship.

Elvis went out of his way to make me feel especially welcome, and to let everybody know that I was his special guest and close friend. Graceland had just been remodeled, and Elvis personally took me on a complete tour of the house. I was told that Elvis spent about $200,000 on renovations and additions. In 1958, that was a bundle of money. The place looked like a million-dollar mansion.

I will describe my favorite rooms, but mere words have limitations, and seeing is better for believing. The living room and dining room were at the front of the mansion to either side of a large entrance foyer. The living room, to the right, had long, white velvet couches down each wall that held your attention until you noticed the tremendous baby grand piano in solid white, trimmed in gold. The drapes were also white and inlaid with gold threads. The matching white shag carpet was so thick I nearly lost sight of my shoes. This decor carried over into the equally impressive dining room on whose walls hung expensive paintings illuminated by the most gorgeous chandelier I had ever seen.

A lovely winding staircase covered with red carpet wound from the foyer to the master bedroom and several other guest bedrooms. The master bedroom suite was sensational with deep, navy blue shag carpet, a tremendous white king-size bed, and built-in telephones, intercom, and a closed-circuit television.

Off the master bedroom were a beautiful study and a large bathroom with mirrors everywhere. It would be several more years before I would see some of the things in other homes that Elvis had in his bedroom. Looking back, the decor reminded me of the movie *2001: A Space Odyssey*.

The playroom and den were downstairs and apparently covered the entire length and most of the width of the main floor. A pool table stood in the middle of the playroom and the walls were almost completely covered with Elvis' gold records. Each gold record was in a frame and had been presented to Elvis by RCA after one of his hits sold 500,000 copies. I counted several gold records hanging on his walls, and Elvis had only been on the national music scene for two years! There were five gold records in one large frame which represented the five million copies that "Heartbreak Hotel" had sold.

The den resembled something in a plush movie theater, only more comfortable. Among the toys in this room were Elvis' 16-mm automatic, push-button controled projector with a hideaway movie screen. There was also a complete ice cream and soda fountain like you would find in a fancy drugstore. In 1958, probably my old penpal Ike Eisenhower lacked such touches in the White House.

It took Elvis about an hour to give me the grand tour. I then called my family to tell them I was on my way.

Elvis could easily have dispatched somebody else to drive me, but he insisted on doing it himself, and went out the back gate of Graceland through a big field. We got in another one of his many limousines — this one a black Cadillac. Apparently, Elvis used the back exit quite often since it was always a hassle to pass through the crowded front gate. Two of his friends, Red West and Lamar Fike, went with us.

West was at the tail end of his own stint in the Marines, but was also currently on a two-week leave. Elvis had known Red from earlier days when both attended Humes High. Red was a talented boxer who was also an all-state football player. He had taken an instant liking to Elvis and protected him from school bullies. In 1955, when Elvis toured with the Blue Moon Boys, Red joined the group as driver and bodyguard. Red was the strong silent type, and obviously viewed me with much skepticism.

Fike had tried to join the Army when Elvis was drafted, but got turned down for medical reasons. He was overweight and not in the best physical shape. Lamar had met Elvis when he was hanging around recording studios. Lamar was taken by Elvis' unusual clothing style and winning personality. They struck up a lasting friendship based on mutual loyalty and playful banter.

My parents thought Elvis was a thoroughly polite and charming young man. His celebrity status didn't impress them as much as his good manners. Elvis was a good sport and let my mother take some candid photos. Before he drove away, Elvis asked me to spend a few days of my 14-day leave with him at Graceland before going back to Fort Hood. This way we could travel back to Fort Hood together. I eagerly accepted his offer and thanked him immensely for everything.

When I arrived home with my family back in Dresden, I discovered I was a celebrity of sorts myself. The hometown folks had seen a lot of photographs of Elvis and I together in the Army. The local weekly newspaper, the *Dresden Enterprise*, had been running articles about my being drafted and stationed with Elvis, and reported that we had become Army buddies. Everybody wanted to know the skinny on Elvis, and frankly their curiosity left me drained. Complete strangers were appearing at my doorstep pumping me for information.

"Tell me all about Elvis."

"What's he like?"

"Can you get his autograph for me?"

"Can you take me to Graceland to meet him?"

I was beginning to understand just how crazy people were about Elvis. It also made me feel sorry for him, in a way, and helped me understand a little more how Elvis must have felt all the time.

I spent that first week of leave at home with my family and catching up on their lives. The second week I spent with Elvis at Graceland, partly because I couldn't get any rest at home answering questions from people seeking information about Elvis, but also because Elvis wanted me to spend time with him at his mansion, which was simply an offer I couldn't refuse.

I was on top of the world. Up to this point, the most important person I had ever met was the mayor of Dresden. Now the King of Rock and Roll was one of my best friends.

My brother Doyle and his son, Mike, came with me back to Memphis in my parents' car, a blue 1957 Impala Chevrolet. As we approached Graceland, the scene at the gate hadn't changed. There were hundreds of people, mostly female, hanging around for a glimpse of their idol.

I wasn't sure it would be easy for us to get through, but the crowd slowly parted as I drove up to the musical gates. It was my luck that Elvis' Uncle Vester was on duty, and as soon as I stuck my head out the driver's side window, he recognized me and opened the gate immediately. The crowd almost audibly swooned at such privilege, but then pressed forward with questions. I ignored them as I drove through the gates quickly so Vester could close it without anyone getting inside or injured.

"Welcome to Graceland, Elvis is expecting you," Uncle Vester smiled. Elvis himself greeted me at the door, saying, "Rexadus, I'm happy you're here, we're gonna have a blast during our last week of leave."

Elvis showed me to the bedroom that I would be staying in, which was right next to his. This room was reserved for the guest of honor, and I was properly flattered.

I quickly got acquainted with the early members of the

"Memphis Mafia." In addition to Lamar and Red there were Alan Fortas; cousins Billy, Gene, and Junior Smith; George Klein; and Nick Adams. Junior was the eldest of the Smith Brothers (all the sons of Mrs. Presley's brother) who died in 1961 from alcohol poisoning. Nick Adams, who later made it big in a TV series called *The Rebel*, also met an untimely death on February 5, 1968, in a freak automobile accident. There were a few others as well.

Instinctively, I could tell they were all busy sizing me up. I was the new member of the group and I sensed their mistrust and resentment. (Later on, I would catch myself harboring similar resentments toward other new friends Elvis would bring on the inside. It was a jealous feeling like maybe Elvis would not pay as much attention to me as the new guy.) But as far as those early Mafioso were concerned, I made up my mind they had better accept me because I was planning to be around for awhile.

Elvis brought me up to date on what he had been up to. There had been an overnight trip to Nashville to record several songs that would be released while he was in Germany. Elvis was pleased with the sessions, but noted that Colonel Parker didn't share his enthusiasm. Those songs included "A Big Hunk o' Love," "I Need Your Love Tonight," "A Fool Such As I," "I Got Stung," and "Ain't That Loving You Baby." He also mentioned that he took his parents to a private screening of *King Creole*, due in theaters July 2, about three weeks away.

I didn't have to wait, however, because Elvis showed the gang *King Creole* on his 16-mm projector in the den at Graceland, which also doubled as his own private movie theater. I thought the movie was fantastic, and I could sense Elvis was also high-spirited about it, too. Decades later, most critics agree that his performance in *King Creole* was his finest on film.

45

To avoid being mobbed, Elvis remained indoors as much as possible throughout the day. Nighttime was for playing, and we all went on Elvis' schedule. The typical day usually began around 4 p.m. with breakfast. Then he would go down to the gate between 5 and 6 o'clock to sign autographs. I even tagged along to help Lamar and Red control the crowds.

Then the fun and games would begin. It included watching movies, ordering pizzas, making milkshakes and playing pool. A few nights later, Elvis rented out the Rainbow Rollerdome skating rink after it closed at midnight, and we caroused there all night long. Red, Billy and Gene Smith, Lamar, and some of the other guys turned the play into a knock-down, drag-out roller derby. Even a few of the girls got involved in the horseplay. Red, being the roughest in the group, would always be the guy to knock most of the people down. It reminded me of ice hockey, but it was all in fun. Elvis was right smack in the middle, loving every minute of it. He enjoyed being surrounded by his close friends and family, which made it especially hard for him when we had to leave the next morning.

The road trip back to Fort Hood in Elvis' shiny, new red Lincoln was somber and disheartening. Not only were we exhausted, but also felt as though we had nothing to look forward to. Elvis was depressed and unusually reserved.

Sadly, Elvis' life was soon going to change forever, and this would be the general mood of times to come.

CHAPTER FIVE

Advanced Basic

We returned to Fort Hood for eight more weeks of what the Army called "advanced basic training." This meant that we were going to learn to be tankers.

We were being trained according to our Military Order Status, or MOS. This number, which goes in your military record, determines what your job specialty is in the Army, or what you have been trained to do.

All soldiers who are trained to be tankers start out with a basic 130.00 MOS. As we advanced in our training to a higher level, our MOS would advance accordingly. When Elvis was discharged, his MOS had advanced to 133.60. The 133 indicated he was trained in armor, but his job was to be scout for his battalion. The 60 indicated he had advanced from a recruit at induction to Sergeant E-5 at the point of discharge.

When I was discharged, my MOS was armor 131.60, meaning I was a tank commander (131) and a Sergeant E-5. A soldier's MOS indicated to your company commander what specific qualifications you had and how you could best serve your outfit, and your country.

We were being trained on the M-48, 90-mm Gun Tank. This tank was also named the "Patton Tank," after the famous general himself. It weighed 50 tons and cost the U.S. Government $250,000 each in the 1950s. This tank had more than pulled its weight in World War II. Following the attack on Pearl Harbor, the American forces finally joined their allies in Europe to help fight Hitler's Army. The German Panzer divisions were all equipped with 78-mm gun tanks, and the Americans had 70-mm guns on their tanks. The German tanks, also known as Tiger tanks, could out-fire our tanks more or less, and run over our tank positions on the battleground. When our 90-mm gun tank was introduced into combat, the tide turned as the Germans could not compete with our bigger guns. Even "Old Blood and Guts," General Patton, was more confident with that kind of advantage.

Advanced basic training would provide us with everything we needed to know about this tank inside and out. Again, the Army gave us the best of everything.

First, we learned how to maintain our tanks in field and battle conditions, which included replacing any damaged section of track. This was back-breaking work that required the full physical strength of all four crew members and skill beyond what we thought possible. The tracks were the hardest part of the tank to maintain because of their weight and strength. It seemed impossible that four men could break apart the track, install a new section, and remount the track to the tank wheels, yet the Army had it down to a science through many years of experience.

We spent days mastering the tank radio system. We learned all the radio communication procedures, including our call signs, how to talk over the radio, how to use the helmet mikes and speakers, how to tune the radio to different channels, and how to maintain the tank radio system.

Every crew member, including the tank commander, the gunner, the loader, and the driver, had to be familiar with everything about the tank. Each of us had to understand and know how to perform the four jobs on the tank until they became second nature. Everyone had the opportunity to drive the tanks and learn all about the big V-12 Chrysler engines. We trained in driving these tanks until it was like driving our own car.

Next, everyone had to learn about the different kinds of ammunitions carried on the tanks and how to fire the guns. Each tank had an allotted amount of ammo rounds for the various guns which included the main 90-mm gun, the 50-caliber, and the two 30-caliber machine guns. In addition to the tank guns, each tanker had a 30-caliber carbine automatic rifle and an Army issue .45 automatic pistol complete with holster and waist strap. Every soldier had to be proficient in the knowledge and use of each one of these weapons. We were timed and tested on a regular basis on how fast we could break down each one, and then clean and reassemble it back into firing order. At the end of our training we had to be able to do it blindfolded.

We spent a lot of time on the firing range during advanced basic. Usually, our mornings consisted of our daily dozen exercises and marching to various classrooms for instructions. The afternoon was spent learning hands-on in the field with all phases of the tanks, their weapons, and battle formations.

Elvis loved working with the tanks and joked that they reminded him of his cherished Cadillacs — same size, weight, and cost! When Elvis was put in command of a tank, he developed a reputation for working his fellow recruits to the bone.

Elvis became a great soldier. He loved the Army and it became a way for him to express himself and find out who he really was.

Meanwhile, Vernon and Gladys Presley, along with Grandma

Minnie Mae Presley, Lamar Fike, the Smith Cousins, Nick Adams, and the others, moved into a three-bedroom trailer home near the base. Elvis had arranged a deal with Stylemaster Mobile Homes to use the trailer for free in exchange for photographs of himself and his family living comfortably in the unit. That lasted only about 10 days, as all the inhabitants were packed in there like sardines.

Elvis then arranged a deal to lease a home from Judge Chester Crawford for $1,500 per month on Oak Hill Drive in nearby Killeen. The house was nothing special, just a three-bedroom, 2,000 square foot, ordinary one-story home. In no time, however, it became a major tourist attraction as word got out who was living there. Crowds appeared right after they settled in and waited for Elvis to get home from the base almost every day.

The move to off-base was actually decided on while Elvis was home on leave. Elvis was permitted to live off post as long as his family was now with him. Did I think it odd that a grown man would bring his family wherever he went? Nope. I would have done the same thing if I had the means. Had he stayed on post, Elvis would never have had a moment of privacy. This was perfectly legal and in accordance with Army regulations. Since basic training was completed, any other GI could have done the same. However, an overwhelming majority of the guys were like me and could not afford to bring their families there for such a short period of time. We would only be in Fort Hood for three more months.

Elvis often escaped to the Dallas/Fort Worth area for some weekend fun. It was usually the four of us — Elvis, Lamar, Norvell, and me. Those trips were therapeutic for all of us, but especially for Elvis. They were his emotional release and helped him to feel like he was still a part of the world.

While in Fort Worth, we stayed at a Quality Inn Motel, where, not surprisingly, everything centered on meeting girls. The main attraction at this particular motel was the large number of airline stewardesses who stayed there. There is nothing wrong with left-overs, which is what we got after Elvis picked his girl. I could never understand where the seemingly endless stream of beautiful girls came from, but they were always there.

When not in Dallas or Fort Worth, we traveled 50 miles to Waco to visit the home of Eddie Fadal. Eddie was a disc jockey who promoted Elvis' early records and helped him break into the Texas radio market. Fadal actually quit his disc jockey position to tour with Elvis in January 1956. After the tour, they lost touch until Eddie heard the news that Elvis would be at Fort Hood for basic training. He went to the base but couldn't get past security until he flashed a picture of Elvis and him together. Elvis was overjoyed to see Eddie again and gave him a big hug. They had a reunion at a nearby Dairy Queen. Eddie gave Elvis a permanent invitation to spend weekends at his house, and offered him all the creature comforts of home. Soon thereafter, Elvis extended the invitation to his friends. Eddie and his wife, Lanelle, were gracious and never did seem to mind the extra company.

We could always count on good food and good fun at the Fadal household. We played records, sang with Elvis around the piano, and watched movies. Eddie was a great host and would wait on us like we were kings. Elvis thought of Eddie as a good friend who would go out of his way to please him and his friends. Eddie and Lanelle had two small children — a beautiful daughter named Janice and a younger son named Dana. While we enjoyed being with Eddie and his family, our hangout of choice was the Quality Inn in Fort Worth. We changed hotels after someone recommended the Sheraton-Dallas Hotel as a place where a lot of girls stayed over. I remember with a cringe what happened when we drove to this particular Sheraton to check out the amenities.

We arrived at the front entrance in Elvis' limousine and asked the doorman if there were any vacant rooms. The doorman was a young man who was fresh on the job. He asked us in return if we had any baggage. We said "No" and wondered why that was so important.

"No bags, no room," said the young man. The doorman obviously didn't recognize Elvis because he was behind the wheel, while Lamar and I did all the talking.

"Let's get the hell out of here if they don't want our business," Elvis said, pitching a fit. "The hell with them!" This was the first time I had ever seen Elvis get mad. He didn't impose his celebrity status on anyone, but at the same time, he was nobody's doormat.

Lamar and I quickly jumped out of the car and asked this young, naive doorman if he really knew what he was doing.

"You just turned down Elvis Presley," I said under my breath. "Do you want to change your mind quickly before you get into trouble?" Naïveté turned out to be the least of this bureaucrat's problems; he was apparently just plain ignorant of who Elvis Presley was. When he still wouldn't relent, we left. Man, did that get ol' Elvis steamed. He pulled out of that hotel so fast the tires seemed to squeal for five minutes.

Within a few weeks, Elvis showed us a letter from the president of the Sheraton Corporation apologizing for the haughty treatment we received and inviting us back to the Dallas Sheraton. Not only were we invited to stay there, but our accommodations would be absolutely free for as long as we wished to partake of the hotel's hospitality. And, the letter went on, we wouldn't have to worry about that dumbbell doorman, either, because he'd been fired. But we never did go back there. Elvis had too much pride.

It didn't take Elvis long to discover the American Airlines Stewardess College in Fort Worth, the country's first and only such facility. Like a good bloodhound, Elvis had an uncanny nose for finding the goods. On one of our weekend trips, Elvis was invited to visit the school, and of course, he issued an invitation to his buddies to come along with him.

As we drove up to the front door of the school in one of Elvis' limousines, we were greeted by a throng of stewardesses, some of whom opened our doors. The house mother actually announced on a P.A. system that Elvis was arriving. Then we were escorted by this beautiful entourage of young ladies to the center of a huge lobby where more than a hundred beautiful women were waiting. It was a scene in the movies. Our own private harem! The action was hard to believe and, again, second choice seemed like filet mignon to me. I had my pick of all but one of all these gorgeous women. I was having the time of my life, I thought, and I did not think there was anything wrong with how I was behaving. I only thought I was sowing my wild oats in a way I never dreamed possible before that time.

Did I think these girls liked me for myself, or just because I was with Elvis? When you're in that situation, you don't even ask that question. You just go with the flow.

That night, several of the girls ended up going back to the hotel with us. We had a great all-night party and Elvis ended up with two of the most beautiful ladies in his room. During the next week Elvis and I would joke with each other about the "hard duty" he pulled in Fort Worth.

But there was no laughter around the first part of August,

when word came that Gladys Presley was ill. She hadn't been feeling well the whole summer, dealing with depression and a continuous loss of appetite. In addition to this, she had a weight problem (Gladys had been taking diet pills on and off for some time) and a drinking problem.

Doctors diagnosed her problem as an undiagnosed liver ailment. Her illness was serious enough that the senior Presleys returned by train to Memphis so Gladys could be cared for by her family doctor, Dr. Charles Clarke, at Methodist Hospital.

Elvis felt desperate to be by his mother's side. He had just finished Advanced Tank Training, but the Army was reluctant to grant Elvis any leave time. His first request was denied. As Gladys' condition declined, her doctor notified the Fort Hood base military personnel office. But fearing the public would view it as special treatment of its prize celebrity, the Army still did nothing. After threatening to go AWOL, Elvis was granted emergency leave on August 12. He flew from Fort Worth to Memphis and spent almost every minute at the hospital. Unfortunately, when Elvis went home to freshen up, Gladys passed away after suffering a heart attack on August 14, 1958. She was only 46.

Elvis called Sergeant Norwood, our company First Sergeant, shortly after her death. They spoke together for about three hours. We all felt sorry for Elvis because we knew how much he loved his mother. She was the most important person in his life. She truly loved and worshipped her only son. She believed that Elvis was blessed with a double dose of talent because of the death of Jesse, Elvis' twin, who was stillborn.

What do you say or how do you comfort a guy who just lost his mother? I hurt with him and let him know I cared. "Elvis, I know you're hurting right now," I said cautiously when Elvis first came

U. S. ARMY RECRUITING MAIN STATION
P. O. BOX 6287
MEMPHIS 11, TENNESSEE

SPECIAL ORDERS   24 March 1958
NUMBER   59   E X T R A C T

    1. Fol named EM having been inducted 24 March 1958 in AUS Unassigned
in Gr of Pvt-El for a pd of 24 mos, MOS 0006 are asgd 24 March 1958 to
4071 SU, Pers Center, Fort Chaffee, Arkansas, WP 24 March 1958 rept to CO
thereat NLT 2400 hrs 24 March 1958 for processing and asgmt.

NAME	SERIAL NUMBER
Moore, Alex E.	US 53 310 760
Presley, Elvis A.	US 53 310 761
Hern, Louis C.	US 53 310 762
Guy, Farley R.	US 53 310 763
Wiggison, Nathaniel (NMN)	US 53 310 764
Maharrey, Robert L.	US 53 310 765
Payne, James Jr.	US 53 310 766
Montague, William C.	US 53 310 767
Christopher, Timothy Jr.	US 53 310 768
Daniel, Gilmore	US 53 310 769
Mansfield, Donald R.	US 25 255 673
Hoover, Wallace J.	US 24 883 433
Norvell, William R.	US 25 347 005

TO will furnish transportation in kind and one meal ticket and one estra
meal ticket from Memphis, Tennessee to Fort Chaffee, Arkansas. WP TDN
PCS 2182010 801-4 P1311-02 S99-999. Auth: Cir 59, Third U. S. Army 57.
This is a group travel order as defined in AR 310-25.

    FOR THE COMMANDER:

OFFICIAL: R. O. FIGUEROA
                                            1st Lt   Inf
                                            Induction Officer

R. O. FIGUEROA
1st Lt., Infantry
Induction Officer

Distribution:
    5 ea CO, 4071 SU, Fort Chaffee, Arkansas
    1 ea Postal Officer
    1 ea EM in Order
    1 ea File

Induction orders in March 1958 when Rex and Elvis were drafted into the Army.

Other Inductees named on page 13 were listed on different Special Orders because their serial

numbers began with RA or FR.

Roy "Cuz" Fisher with Elvis (wearing his multi-colored coat) at Fisher's Steak House in March 1958. Elvis was on his way to Fort Chaffee, Arkansas on the day of his induction. (courtesy of Roy and Chee Chee Fisher)

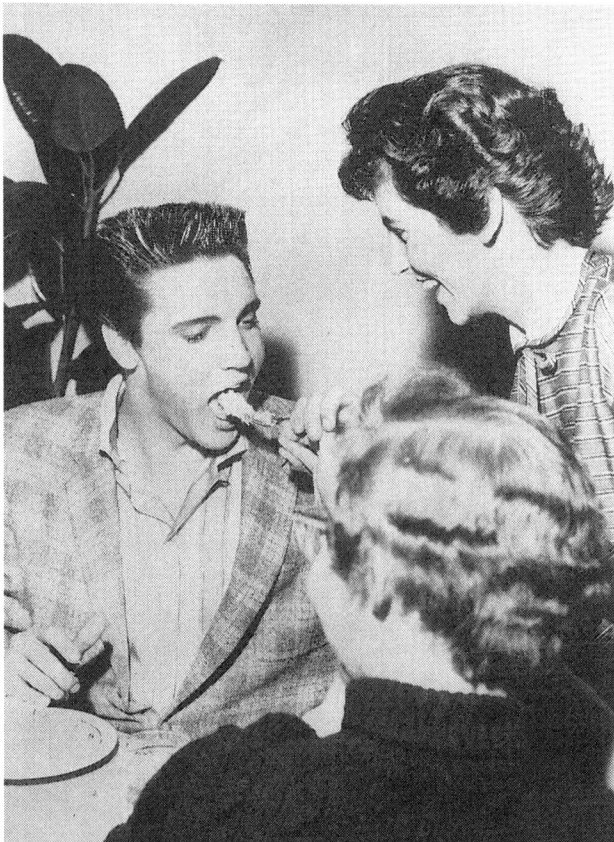

In March 1958, Chee Chee Fisher feeds cake to Elvis at Fisher's Steak House, while the woman (name unknown) seated at the table was president of Elvis' Memphis fan club. The fan club followed his bus from Memphis. (courtesy of Roy and Chee Chee Fisher)

Left: Bill "Nervous" Norvell and Elvis on guard duty

Below: Elvis and Sergeant Wallace on guard duty

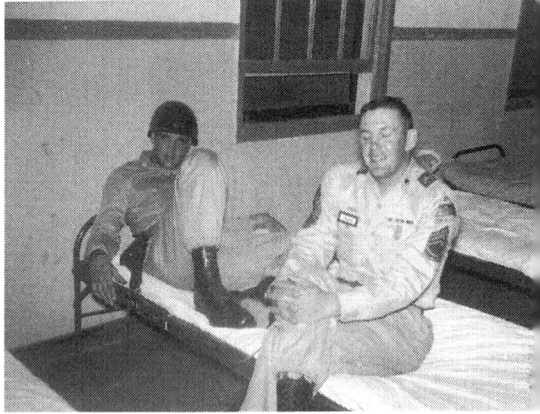

Left: Elvis on guard duty during basic training

Below: Sergeant Wallace (hand raised) stands in front of Elvis Presley and Rex Mansfield during guard duty.

Anita Wood with Elvis (courtesy of the estate of Eddie and Lanelle Fadal)

Elvis behind the wheel with Anita Wood (courtesy of the estate of Eddie and Lanelle Fadal)

Elvis standing next to his car and waving farewell to Rex's family

The Graceland Mansion with Rex's car

Rex getting out of the car at Graceland

Rex's family meets the King.

Elvis giving autographs to Rex's family

Elvis leaves in his car after delivering Rex to his family.

Anita Wood, Elvis, and Eddie and Lanelle Fadal
(courtesy of the estate of Eddie and Lanelle Fadal)

Elvis with Eddie Fadal at the Fadal home in Waco, Texas (courtesy of the estate of Eddie and Lanelle Fadal)

Close-up of Elvis wearing his Army cap and uniform (courtesy of the estate of Eddie and Lanelle Fadal)

A bedroom in the house that Elvis rented for himself and his parents during "advanced basic training" in Killeen, Texas

Living room in the house in Killeen

Kitchen in the Killeen house

This house that Elvis rented still exists at 609 Oak Hill Drive in Killeen, Texas.

Rex and Elisabeth's son, Don, outside Elvis' old house in Killeen, Texas

Elvis signing autographs

Nick Adams, Eddie Fadal, and Elvis
(courtesy of the estate of Eddie and Lanelle Fadal)

Close-up of Elvis at home in Killeen, Texas (courtesy of the estate of Eddie and Lanelle Fadal)

Elvis in front of the fire-place at his rented home in Killeen (courtesy of the estate of Eddie and Lanelle Fadal)

Group photo of Elvis with family and friends before he left Fort Hood to ship out to Germany (courtesy of the estate of Eddie and Lanelle Fadal)

This photo of Janie Wilbanks was given to Elisabeth ("Liz") shortly after her marriage to Rex. (courtesy of Frank Broden)

Janie Wilbanks

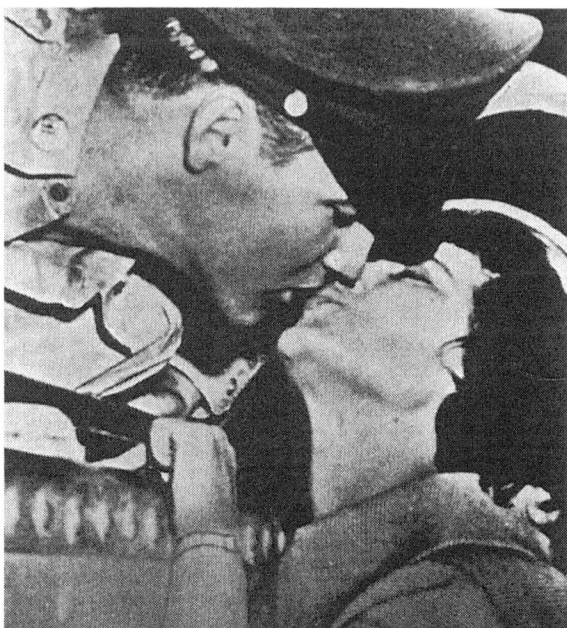

Famous photo of Elvis kissing Janie Wilbanks in Memphis during a train stop from Fort Hood to Brooklyn Harbor, New York (courtesy of George Klein of Memphis)

Photo of train station at Bremerhaven, Germany taken from troop ship in October 1958

Arrival by troop ship at Bremerhaven, Germany

Elvis at Elisabeth's home in Grafenwohr with Linda McCormick (Elisabeth's sister) and neighborhood boy

Elvis at Elisabeth's home with a crowd of neighborhood kids wanting autographs

Elisabeth, Elvis, and a neighbor's daughter

Rex in front of a tank at Grafenwohr, where he first saw Elisabeth (courtesy of Tom Stoddart of Independent Photographers Group, London)

Park Hotel in Bad Neuheim, which was the second place where Elvis stayed off-base

Hotel Grunewald where Elvis rented the entire third floor, plus a room for Elisabeth on the second floor

Photo taken in March 1982 of the front of the rented house in Bad Neuheim, Goethestrasse 14 (courtesy of Radermaker, a German photographer)

Back of the Bad Neuheim house (courtesy of Radermaker)

Elvis with Margit Buergin, his first German girlfriend, and Red West, along with some young German fans outside Ritters Park Hotel, where Elvis first stayed off-base.

Elvis stands with a small crowd in front of his house at Bad Neuheim. (Rex at far right)

Elvis plays football in Bad Neuheim.

Elvis stands in the football
field during a game.

Close-up of Elvis in front of the house

Elvis watches a football game at Ray Barracks.

Elvis stands in front of his house.

The King with his car and house

Elvis walks in front of his car and house.

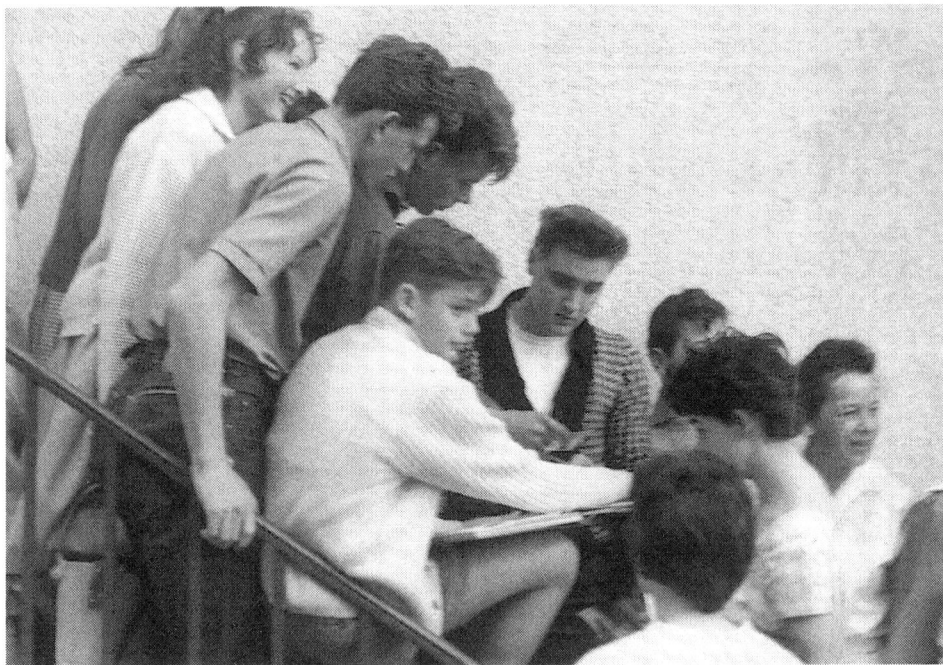

Elvis signs autographs in front of his house in Bad Neuheim.

Elisabeth alone in the office

Elvis reads some fan mail in the office.

Elvis laughing with a cigar in hand and Rex with his back turned and going out the door

Charlie, Lamar, Elvis, and Rex (laughing), in front of the house with a dog

Elvis lounges on his couch in the house.

Autographed photo of Elvis playing the guitar was given personally to Elisabeth in 1959

Dee Stanley and Grandma Minnie Mae Presley at the home in Bad Neuheim

Charlie Hodge, Lamar Pike, Elisabeth, and George Young at a club in the Bad Neuheim area

Elvis in his jeep with a German and an American soldier (courtesy of U.S. Army)

Elvis in his jeep with two German soldiers (courtesy of U.S. Army)

Elvis looks through binoculars as a scout. (courtesy of U.S. Army)

Headquarters Company barracks in Friedberg, Germany, where Elvis reported for duty each day

Elvis reads mail in his barracks.
(courtesy of U.S. Army)

back, "but I want you to know I'm here for you if you need me."

"Rexadus, I knew I could count on you," Elvis said, wiping away a tear. Those were the only words I said to him about his mother's passing. I preferred to let him know I cared more by my actions and willingness to spend time with him, allowing him to talk freely about his mother when he felt like it.

Elvis was allowed to stay a few extra days in Memphis on compassionate leave to attend his mother's funeral. Lamar told me later that Elvis wept so hard it made his skin crawl. He added that when Gladys' casket was lowered into the ground at the gravesite, Elvis completely lost it. At her funeral he had to be physically restrained by those in attendance, who feared he might jump down in her grave where she lay in her closed casket.

Elvis returned to Fort Hood on August 24. His family and close friends came back to the house on Oak Hill Drive soon afterwards to comfort him during his grieving period. Anita Wood and Colonel Parker stopped by frequently to check in on Elvis.

Things were never quite the same again at Fort Hood after Gladys' death. Elvis' demeanor noticeably changed. Before he was happy-go-lucky, but now he was grief-stricken and much more serious. The whole outfit suffered with and for Elvis' great loss. It was a somber time as we finished the rest of our training.

After advanced basic we went into another advanced training program which would last about four weeks. During our final week, Elvis was promoted to private first-class. This helped to build up his spirit and self-esteem.

During the final four weeks, we continued the same training as the previous eight weeks of advanced basic. The Army was great at going over and over the same stuff until you were bored stiff and could do it blindfolded. They say you can only appreciate the reason for it if and when you have to use it facing the enemy on the battlefield. We bitched a lot about the boredom, but down deep we understood it was necessary.

On September 11th, we finally received our orders telling us when and where we would be shipped to serve our country for the remainder of our military hitch. We were going to West Germany.

We discovered we would serve in the 3rd Armored Division of the 7th Army, also called the Spearhead Division. Its motto was "Victory or Death."

Elvis spent his last night in Texas at Eddie Fadal's house with Anita Wood, and he was at the most vulnerable point in his life. He expressed to Eddie his deepest fears. "Eddie, I really feel this is the end of my career. Everybody is going to forget about me," he said.

He was wrong as he could be, of course, but who knew? At least we would be getting out of that blazing Texas heat. Maybe a change in temperature and scenery would do us all good.

CHAPTER SIX

The Trek to Germany

We boarded the troop train at Ford Hood on September 19, 1958, and headed for Brooklyn, New York. There were 1,360 well-trained GI's on that train and we were being shipped over to Germany as replacements. Our objective was to defend a portion of the Western side of the East-West German border. The entire mission sounded very exciting to all of us. Most of us had never been overseas before, including Elvis.

On the way to New York, our train stopped briefly in Memphis. Absolutely no one was allowed to get off. Naturally, the fans found out where Elvis was and the rail yard in Memphis was flooded. It was almost as if the Army was giving the hometown fans a final look at their idol before sending him away to Germany. But Uncle Sam isn't the sentimental kind, and the big crowd and all the reporters were most likely the handiwork of Colonel Tom Parker, who always worked every angle to get his boy as much publicity as possible.

It was at the Memphis stop where Elvis first met Janie Wilbanks. She was an enchanting, dark-haired beauty from New Albany, Mississippi. In the midst of the crowd, Janie recognized George Klein, a Memphis disc jockey, host of *Rock 'N' Roll Ballroom*, and a friend of Elvis'. She realized then she was in the right place at the right time and remained close to where Klein stood waiting. With Klein was Alan Fortas, another good friend of Elvis'. When the train stopped right in front of them, Elvis couldn't help but notice Janie and asked his buddies about her. Then he did more.

"Well, put her up on the steps," Elvis requested.

Klein and Fortas gave Janie a boost, and suddenly she was face to face with Elvis. Elvis leaned out of the train, held Janie's face with both hands, and gently kissed her a few times. As surprised as she was, she still managed to introduce herself.

"My name is Jane Davis Wilbanks, and I'm from New Albany," she told Elvis.

"I won't forget you," Elvis replied. A picture was taken when they kissed, and this famous photo made newspapers around the globe, immortalizing this moment in pop-culture history forever.

Later, Elvis called Klein and asked him to tell Janie to write to him in Germany. Klein gave Janie the address, she wrote, and informed Elvis that before Christmas, she would visit him in Germany. Coincidentally, she had an uncle stationed in Kassel who was a Chaplain in the Army. This gave her an excuse to make the long trip.

Elvis, Norvell, and I were in the same train car headed for New York. We talked about spending the next two years in Germany, and about the 10-day ocean voyage that would take us there. We all looked forward to the adventure, although Elvis still seemed worried about his temporary absence from the entertainment industry. He was also still grieving for his mother. I believe this is when God reached out and comforted Elvis by sending him someone who could make him laugh easily.

"Where's Elvis? I gotta see this guy!" this pint-sized GI yelled aloud in the train car. He introduced himself as Charlie Hodge.

He and Elvis had actually met before backstage in Memphis during a gospel concert. Charlie was with a gospel quartet, the Foggy River Boys, and appeared weekly on the ABC network.

Elvis didn't recognize Hodge in his uniform and crewcut, but spoke to him anyway.

"Hey, you look familiar," Elvis said.

"I'm Charlie. I was the lead singer with the Foggy River Boys."

"Hey man, I used to watch you on TV every Saturday night," said Elvis.

"You used to watch me?" Charlie asked, astounded that Elvis had noticed him.

The two men hit it off right away. Charlie was a hoot and had a booming laugh for such a small guy. Charlie's smile and sense of humor were disarming. He told us jokes and stories, talked about the folks he knew in the gospel music field, and kept us in stitches for hours on end. He was from Alabama, so we shared a common bond — all coming from the South.

This was a hard time for Elvis, and Charlie was a breath of fresh air. On the ship to Germany, Elvis requested that Charlie share his compartment with him. Charlie was with Elvis until the day he died. Like I said, he was a godsend.

We arrived at the Military Ocean Terminal at Brooklyn Harbor on the morning of September 22, 1958. About 200 reporters and photographers were on hand and the Army permitted them to interview Elvis for a couple of hours. It was Elvis' final press conference before his departure overseas.

"Elvis, since you've been in the Army, have the boys given you kind of a rough time and embarrassed you because of your past career, would you say?" one reported asked.

"No sir," Elvis said. "I was very surprised, I never met a better group of boys in my life. They probably would have if it had been like everybody thought. I wouldn't have to work and I would be given special treatment, and this and that. But when they looked around and saw that I was on KP, and pulling guard and everything, just like they were, well they figured, he's just like us."

With a borrowed duffel bag in tow, Elvis walked the gangplank several times so that photographers could get the quintessential shot of a soldier going off to serve his country. In the background a military band was playing their own version of "Tutti Frutti," which made everything even more surreal. I guess they thought he was Little Richard.

"In spite of the fact that I'm going away and I'll be out of their eyes for some time, I hope I'm not out of their minds. And I'll be looking forward to the time when I can come back and entertain again like I did," Elvis said referring to his fans, in his closing remarks to the press.

In the meantime, the rest of us were boarding the USS *Randall*, a military ship that had clearly seen better days. This was not going to be a luxury cruise across the Atlantic. Once aboard, we all stood on the deck above the gangplank so we could have a bird's-eye view of Elvis and the media frenzy going on around him.

The press conference and photo session did not delay our departure too much. The military band played "Don't Be Cruel" as Elvis walked up the gangplank, and then we set sail for Bremerhaven, Germany.

The sailing time to Bremerhaven was normally 10 days with good weather. For most of us, it was our very first sailing experience, and many got seasick. The Atlantic Ocean can be very rough during bad weather, and this trip was no exception. Some of the guys were nicknamed "Canvas Back" because the minute they stepped foot on the ship until the minute they stepped off, all they could do was lay flat on their backs on their canvas bunks and be sick 24 hours a day. Our bunk beds were stacked up five high. If you were on the bottom bunk — look out!

Elvis and I were among the lucky few who did not get seasick. It was a standard joke among the lucky ones to be asked, "Hey soldier, where are you going?" In response, you would stick your head over the side of the ship and yell back, "Euuuuuuuuuurope!" This was supposed to approximate the sound of vomiting.

Life aboard the ship was busy. We had daily instructions from information officers concerning what our job duties would entail in Germany, and what was expected of us as soldiers.

In our downtime, we watched the latest movies on a 16-mm projector and played lots of cards. Crazy Eight was the ship favorite. Interestingly enough, I never once saw Elvis participate in any of these floating card games. Later on, I learned that Elvis didn't gamble because he wanted to remain true to his public persona and be a positive role model for young people, but that sure didn't apply to Colonel Tom Parker.

But Elvis was a major factor in one of the liveliest forms of entertainment for the GI's during our crossing. It was a live show using whatever talent was aboard. Elvis was appointed the producer and director. He did not entertain the troops himself, but helped organize the so-called talent show. There were auditions conducted by Elvis with those who had (or thought they had) musical talent. Finalists were selected. Elvis did actually play the piano and guitar for some of the acts, but he was never in the spotlight. I believe the Colonel had laid down the law on what Elvis could and could not do in the area of entertainment while in the Army.

"Elvis, my boy, don't give away entertainment for nothing; it's worth too much to give it away for free," I can hear the Colonel saying. Most performers went into the Special Services in the military, utilizing their talents to entertain the troops. But the Colonel expressly steered Elvis away from that. This way, he figured Elvis would gain more public respect by playing it straight and pulling regular duty like any other GI. In retrospect, there is absolutely no doubt that their plan worked to perfection.

The talent show turned out to be a nice diversion for Elvis from the devastation he felt over the death of his mother. Elvis was placed in special quarters on the ship, for privacy issues, and he bunked with Charlie Hodge. Charlie also assisted with coordinating the talent show, which helped to cheer up Elvis.

"I used to hear Elvis grieving in his bunk at night; it was less than a month since he'd lost his mother," Charlie said. Another soldier gave Elvis a book of *Poems That Touch the Heart.* The book provided him with a sense of serenity during that time of sorrow.

The live show was presented shortly before we reached our destination. Elvis did a great job putting it together. It was comprised of many talented people, including Charlie, who served as emcee and played piano for some of the acts. The troops really enjoyed every minute of the production. We gave Elvis a long standing ovation for his part in directing the show. Everyone, myself included, was really proud of Elvis and the performers for staging such a quality production.

When we arrived at the mouth of the English Channel, we saw the famous White Cliffs of Dover. They were a beautiful sight to behold. The cliffs looked especially good to us since we had not seen land for about 10 days. An English pilot navigated our ship through the Channel.

The following morning, October 1, 1958, we arrived in Bremerhaven, Germany, and were loaded onto a German troop train.

Bremerhaven was at the time Germany's biggest North Sea coastal town, Europe's most important fishing port, an international trading center, a shipbuilding location, and one of Germany's largest cruise ship ports.

Newsreel cameramen and several press photographers joined hundreds of screaming German fans, mostly teenage girls, waiting at our port. They were held back by ropes and the Military Police forming a human fence.

The fans were so far back from the ship that they could get only a glimpse of Elvis at the most, but this did not seem to discourage them. Elvis was caught off guard by this display, because he had no idea he had such loyal fans in Germany. All of a sudden he realized his celebrity status reached far and went beyond the boundaries of his native country.

Before he boarded the troop train to Friedberg, Elvis revealed to a reporter his feelings of the moment.

"I was very surprised at the reception. I wasn't expecting anything quite that big and I only regret that I didn't have more time to stay there with them. But maybe someday I can come back, when my Army tour is up, as an entertainer, and then I'll have more time, and maybe an opportunity to kind of make myself at home here. Thank you very much. Arrivederci." Then Elvis paused for a second and laughed. "Oh, that's Italian, isn't it?"

Soon we began the final leg of our trip and traveled 200 miles to Ray Barracks, home of "Spearhead," the 32nd Battalion, in Friedberg, Germany. Friedberg is located about 30 miles from Frankfurt. We arrived at about 7:30 p.m., and once again there was a crowd of fans outside the base to greet Elvis. They never got to see him, though, because our troop train entered the Kaserne through a back gate where no civilians were permitted.

Man, it was a dreary looking place. Of course, no Army post will be confused with the Ritz-Carlton, but Ray Barracks was a real downer. The thick layer of fog over everything didn't help matters. We would soon understand that the fog was a constant weather condition in Germany, especially in the winter.

The best way to describe our new home for the next 17 months is "minimal." Our battalion of replacement soldiers stepped off the train and formed into various platoons and companies. As we marched up the main street, we noticed that on our left was the full battalion of 90-mm gun tanks. To our right were open fields that would later be used for target practice and physical training (PT). Next to the tanks on our left was a long gray building that housed both the motor pool and the service area for jeeps and other vehicles.

Across the street in front of the motor pool, on our right, was a line of buildings that we soon learned were our barracks. At the end of the street was the battalion headquarters building, the mess hall, and the non-commissioned officers' (NCO) club. In front of each set of barracks was the company headquarters building which contained the company commander's office and a supply room on the ground floor. The top floor was a recreation room with a few pool tables. Directly behind the company headquarters building were the two-story barracks that became our sleeping quarters.

Graceland it wasn't. The barracks were equipped with the standard Army community showers, latrines, and platoon sergeants' bedrooms.

The bunks were nothing more than steel-framed bunk beds, and the floors were covered with dark gray linoleum. Elvis was assigned to bed 13, but I had a hunch he wouldn't be sleeping there for long.

We were told that the barracks had been the home of Hitler's ss troops during World War II. Now we were going to call it home for the next year-and-a-half. There were several bags of fan mail in Elvis' barracks already waiting for him.

The following day, October 2nd, Elvis attended his final press conference at the Enlisted Men's Canteen before he was officially pronounced off-limits. Ray Barracks brass intended to make a good impression with the media and had the facilities scrubbed and touched-up before the press conference. Right before Elvis met the media, he brushed against a freshly painted area and got paint on his newly pressed uniform. Officials tried to get the stain out, but Elvis ended up reeking of paint remover. Finally, he was issued a new jacket and went out to meet the press.

One of the first questions a reporter asked was if he still hoped to meet the newly engaged Brigitte Bardot, to which he smiled. There was an artillery battalion, an infantry battalion, and our tank battalion in the 3rd Armored Division, along with various support groups assigned to the Friedberg Kaserne. There were other Kasernes (in Germany, Army posts are called Kasernes) in the sur-rounding areas with similar divisions and groups. Most of the troops that came over on the USS *Randall* ended up in Friedberg or the surrounding areas. The troops that came to Friedberg were split up into the various battalions.

Elvis was originally assigned to D Company, and I was assigned to C Company, both in the 1st Battalion, 32nd Armor, Third Armored Division. Elvis was assigned to be the company commander, Captain Russell's jeep driver, but Russell immediately became frustrated by the hundreds of phone calls and all the fan mail and reporters that surrounded Elvis, so Elvis was moved into the scout platoon of headquarters company.

Elvis was to train to be a Scout for our tanks. The Scouts would go ahead of the tanks to set up roadblocks, direct traffic, give enemy positions, etc. In case of war, the Scouts would be the first to contact the enemy.

Elvis liked his assignment because it made his outfit the leader of the pack. Ira Jones was his Platoon Sergeant and a good match for Elvis. Jones was an experienced, patient Southern gentleman who had acquired a reputation for becoming a father figure to young soldiers. It was a blessing for Elvis since he had been especially close to Sergeant Bill Norwood.

I became a tank commander in C Company, in one of the headquarters' platoon tanks, which was occasionally used by our company commander. His name was First Lieutenant Patton, reported to be the cousin of General Patton himself. I never did learn his first name, nor did I want to. I don't think any of the GI's in my company would have dared call him by his first name even if we knew what it was. He was tough enough to be "Old Blood and Guts" reincarnated. He would call us out in formation and let us know in no uncertain terms that we were expected to come in no less than first in all battalion inspections, whatever he said was the law, without question.

He was a large man in excellent physical shape, and personally challenged anyone in our company who had a problem with him or his way of doing business to take it up with him with their fists in the back of our barracks. Nobody in our platoon ever took him up on it.

When the press conference ended, the cameras and reporters were no longer welcome. However, I would soon be granted full access to the Presley inner sanctum.

CHAPTER SEVEN

Deutschland

For the first few days in Germany, I didn't see much of Elvis. We were both engrossed in learning our jobs and adapting to the new environment. Elvis was especially busy trying to find a place where he, his family and entourage could live off post. He was temporarily residing with all of the other GI's on base and stayed with us for about three nights, still working hard to be "just one of the guys."

Any time he could get off during the day, Elvis went out looking for a place to live. But every place he went, the landlord wanted to charge him 10 times the normal rental rate because of who he was.

Even before Elvis found a suitable place to live, Vernon, Grandma Minnie, Lamar Fike, and Red West were already in Germany. I was surprised to hear Red had come. Apparently, he had just been discharged from the Marines and came straight over to be with Elvis.

On October 4, 1958, Elvis' family and friends moved into the world-renowned Ritters Park Hotel in Bad Homburg. Elvis visited with them his first weekend off post, and it proved to be a girl-worthy event. When he and Lamar took a stroll in a nearby park, they encountered a cute, young blonde girl accompanied by a well-known photographer. The photographer suggested to Elvis that he pose with the 16-year-old Margit Buergin. Elvis put his arm around her and she looked up and smiled at him. Those pictures were published in newspapers and magazines across the nation and she was cast in the role of Elvis' newest girlfriend. Elvis thought Margit was a dead ringer for Brigitte Bardot and asked the photographer for her name and phone number.

A few days later, the Army gave Elvis permission, under the military sponsoring act, to take up residence off-base. The Presley clan, plus Lamar Fike and Red West, moved into four rooms at the Hilberts Park Hotel in Bad Nauheim, a few miles from Friedberg.

Bad Nauheim was a resort town noted for its salt springs and spa baths, which were said to be helpful in treating heart and nerve diseases. Many people came there for health reasons, usually under a doctor's care, to take hot baths every day in the special mineral waters.

The Hilberts Park Hotel was a place where elderly people went to get treatments for their ailments until it became a playground for Elvis and his boys. The mission was to find things to laugh about, with no regard for other guests staying at the hotel.

The activities included marching up and down the halls like it was boot camp, wrestling matches, generally making a lot of noise, having water fights, and tinkering with the fire extinguishers. Most of these diversions were created by Lamar and Red to keep Elvis from getting too serious about his current circumstances.

It turned out that Elvis was not the only king staying in the hotel. An oil sheik, King ibn-Saud, one of the richest men in the world, was also staying at the Hilberts Park Hotel. The sheik visited Bad Nauheim once a year to enjoy the relaxing spa baths available in town.

Just like Elvis, the sheik had an entourage, only his was much larger and more impressive. Also, they were both generous men. Elvis bought his friends and family members cars. The sheik gave gold watches instead of signing autographs. Unlike Elvis, however, the sheik was a very serious man, as were all the people who surrounded him. He was upset by all the noise and chaos caused by the Presley gang's fun and games. The sheik was also extremely concerned about his beautiful daughter, who had eyes for Elvis. Her stern father would not let his daughter anywhere near the swivel-hipped singer.

The two famous men caused quite a media circus at the hotel. Frankly, Elvis felt threatened by the competition and didn't enjoy sharing the spotlight with the sheik.

My understanding is that Elvis and the gang were finally asked to leave the hotel and never come back. The other guests and staff at the Hilberts Park Hotel never took much of a shine to Elvis & Co., and so the hotel operators gave them the boot. It was more than likely the oil sheik had a hand in their eviction, but Elvis didn't mind because he didn't like the hotel, the food, nor King ibn-Saud.

On October 27, Vernon, Minnie, Red, Lamar, and Elvis moved to the Hotel Grunewald at Terrassenstrasse 10, located just a few blocks up the hill from the Park Hotel. The well-preserved Grunewald, constructed in the nineteenth century, catered to affluent, elderly guests that appreciated its antiquated decor.

In his book, *Elvis: What Happened?* Red West put it not so nicely. "It was sort of an outpatients' hotel for heart-attack victims," he wrote. "There wasn't anyone there under sixty, and every one of them looked like they had one foot in the grave and the other one on a roller skate."

Elvis rented out the entire top floor, which included a four-bedroom apartment with a living room, kitchen, and bathroom, plus one large bedroom on the floor below just to house his piles of fan mail. This eventually became the room where his private secretary resided, becoming a combination bedroom and office. Grandma, Vernon, and Elvis each had separate bedrooms, while Lamar and Red camped out in a small top floor bedroom. When Elvis was on duty, Red and Lamar spent time at Beck's Bar which was around the corner from the hotel.

Herr Otto Schmidt, the proprietor of the Grunewald Hotel, was a pleasant man who befriended Elvis immediately. He granted Elvis the privilege of smoking in his hotel rooms which was verboten for everybody else. The smoking privilege was for Vernon, Lamar, and Red's cigarettes, plus cigars for Elvis. The accommodations were much more to Elvis' liking because of the kitchen. The kitchen was important to Elvis because he craved certain foods. Now Grandma could continue to fix the favorite foods that his mother Gladys had cooked for him all his life.

When it came to Army food, Elvis was like the rest of us. Every GI complained about it. For example, the typical breakfast meal consisted of corned beef and hash on toast, or some unidentifiable meat mixed with gravy and poured over toast. Lunch and dinner were not any better.

His favorite foods included burned bacon, hard fried eggs, Hormel chili without beans, canned peaches, wieners, butter and jelly on toasted white bread, and peanut butter and banana sandwiches. The peanut butter and bananas were mashed and mixed together, spread on white bread and toasted in a frying pan. In the two years I spent with Elvis, I never once saw him eat steak. The guy had no desire for gourmet foods and could eat the same old fare day in and day out.

Minnie Mae was one of those grand people who worked and worked for everybody, and seldom received thanks from anybody. All of the fame and fortune Elvis had achieved didn't concern her in the least. She remained the same ol' country girl with no frills. She was my favorite of the group and I even called her "Grandma" as did Lamar.

While Lamar was instantly liked by everybody, with Red it was a little different. At first I didn't like him much myself. Elvis had always painted this picture to me of Red as a mean, tough dude with a hair-trigger temper. I was apprehensive of him in the beginning, and I think he resented me a bit. It wasn't long before Red softened up toward me and I was fully accepted by all members of this exceptionally close group. Red finally came around and understood I was one of those "chosen" by Elvis.

It felt good to be completely on the inside, but in order to stay on the inside, you had to instinctively know when to keep your mouth shut to outsiders.

I learned an invaluable lesson from a guy named Donald Pettit: Never write or tell any stories about Elvis to the press. Pettit was a fairly good friend going back to Fort Hood. He and Elvis were in the same barracks during basic training, and Pettit was included on some of our weekend trips.

But then Pettit wrote a story after we got to Germany entitled "Elvis in the Army," which was published by *Ideal Magazine*.

The article bragged about how tight Pettit and Elvis had become since entering the Army. There were photographs of him and Elvis wearing squad leader arm bands on their sleeves, and pictures of Pettit's family. I'm sure Pettit was paid a nice fee for his participation in this article, but he certainly paid a bigger price later on. After the article came out, Pettit was completely shunned by Elvis and was never allowed to be part of the inside group again. He was dropped like a hot potato and the fun and games carried on without him.

From the get-go, the Presley party didn't endear itself to the other guests at the Grunewald. Apparently, an elderly lady staying below them always kept a broom within arm's reach. She thumped on the ceiling with the broom and shouted German curse words when she heard noises above her.

History repeated itself as the horseplay, ass-grabbing, pillow fights, wrestling, and constant racket throughout the nights wound up irritating many other guests. Meanwhile, crowds of fans were always lined up in front of the hotel, which made it difficult for guests to get in and out. There were many elderly people, especially women, staying in all the hotels and guest houses in Bad Nauheim. Some of these old gals didn't appreciate Elvis' and his group's aggressive and playful sense of humor.

Elvis invented a game that was extremely painful to the hands. Elvis would watch your hands from the corners of his eyes, and when you were least expecting it, he hit the back of your hand with his knuckles. When you got hit solid, it hurt like hell. Red, Lamar, Elvis, Vernon, and I joined in this game. Some days the backs of our hands were black and blue from the knuckling, but it was still amusing.

We used to play a game called "God," which was not meant in any way to be sacrilegious. In this game, every time a compliment was overheard about anything at all, the listener would say "Thank you."

For instance, "What a beautiful day!" I would innocently exclaim. One of the guys would say "Thank you," as if taking credit for the beautiful day. Elvis would delight at the bewilderment on an outsider's face when we did it in front of him. I played this joke on some of my buddies at the base, and they stared at me like I was crazy. It was a bit strange, I guess, but it helped pass the time.

The owner of the Grunewald soon grew tired and frustrated with Elvis' antics, and their friendship wore thin as events sort of spun out of control. Once Elvis brought a dog named Cherry back to the hotel with him and expected Schmidt and his employees to care for him. Then there was a wrestling match between Red and Lamar which resulted in a broken bed.

The last straw was a shaving-cream war between Red and Elvis that got way out of hand. Elvis locked himself in a bathroom, and Red came up with a sure-fire way to get him out that involved sliding some toilet paper under the door and setting it on fire. Some of the guests saw smoke and were terrified that the building was on fire. We didn't know much German, but we knew "Raus!" meant get out. Vernon began searching full-time for a house they could move into.

While Vernon Presley was often described as cold and aloof, he actually had a terrific sense of humor which carried over to Elvis. The two of them together kept us laughing for hours. They joked around and teased each other constantly. Vernon and his son had invented their own special vocabulary, and once I began to comprehend it, I got in on the act.

Here are some samples of the Presley lexicon:

1. BURNT = When someone said something or did something that hurt Elvis or one of us, which he did not like or appreciate.

2. BURNT TO A CRISP = Much more severe than just burnt.

3. SCALDED = Another word for burnt, but relating to being burned by boiling water or hot grease.

4. SCALDED TO THE BONE = More severe than just scalded.

Vernon enjoyed using the scalded words.

5. CAUGHT = Someone was doing something he was not supposed to be doing and was caught in the act. For example, if Elvis thought one of us guys was looking at one of his girls in what he perceived to be the wrong way, he would say "caught," and we were busted.

6. YOU POOR OL' PITIFUL THING = Something someone said or did that was stupid. In other words, when anyone said or did something Elvis thought was stupid, this was his way of saying he felt sorry for that person. It could also be used as a put-down to confirm stupidity.

The inner group adopted the Presleys' special vocabulary. In one aspect, these terms were an easy way to tell someone you did not like or appreciate what he had said or done, without actually having to confront him directly. It was also a way for Elvis to control the inner group.

Elvis was as generous as he was playful. Captain Edward E. Betts was the Commander of the Headquarters Company to which Elvis was assigned as a scout driver. Betts wanted to buy a BMW, but could never afford it on his salary. When Elvis learned of his Captain's desire, he decided to intervene. Elvis purchased Bett's old beat-up Cadillac from him. From what I understand, Elvis paid a lot more for the Cadillac than it was worth so the Captain would have enough to buy the BMW.

Vernon gave his blessing to this transaction and the Captain was able to obtain his dream car. The Cadillac Elvis purchased was later traded for a black Mercedes-Benz.

Toward the middle of November, 1958, our Battalion went to Grafenwohr for field training. Grafenwohr was, and still is, the main training area in Germany for all U.S. troops, positioned 110 miles from the border of Czechoslovakia (now the Czech Republic). Every American soldier stationed in Germany had to go to Grafen-wohr for special training. The German and American troops took weapons training there at some point.

Our weapon proficiency tests started with the Army .45 Automatic pistol and went up to the 90-mm gun. In between were the grease gun, the carbine, the M-1 rifle, the 30-caliber machine gun, and the 50-caliber machine gun. We carried the Army .45 on our hips and the 90-mm gun was carried by our M-48 tank along with the other weapons. In Grafenwohr, we fired only live ammunition.

While Elvis' bravery was admirable, he confided his true feel-ings about his Grafenwohr experience to Sergeant Bill Norwood in a letter dated November 11, 1959. It was evident that Elvis was raring to get back to performing again, appearing in movies, and, in his words, "the good ol' U.S.A." The letter appears courtesy of owner Rich Consola.

Dear Sgt. Norwood and family,

Well, I'm writing a letter for the first time in years. I received your letter and was glad to hear everything is O.K. I am in a scout platoon and believe me we are on the move all time. We are up at a place called Grafenwohr. I'm sure you've heard of it. It's miserable up here and we are here for six weeks. The German people are very nice and friendly but there is no place like the good ol' U.S.A. I am with a good bunch of boys and Sgt., although I would have given anything to stay at Ft. Hood with you guys. I talked to Anita every so often and she writes me all the time. I sure miss her along with 50 million others — ha. Boy I'll tell you something, I will be so thankful when my time is up. I can get hardly wait to get back home and entertain folks and make movies and everything. Well it will come some day soon. All of us were supported over here. Norvell and Mansfield are in other companies but there is a lot of good boys in this outfit. Well tell Abbey and the kids hello for me. Also tell Sgt. Wallace and Lt. Meister hello for me and if I get a chance I will write to them. Tell Sgt. Wallace to write me sometime so I will know where to write him. Well when it's over we will get together again and it'll be like old times. Well I have to go now so you all take care and write again.

Your Friend
P.F.C. Elvis Presley

I was with Elvis during most of our off-duty time. It was as if he wanted me to be his bodyguard when he was away from Red and Lamar. Since those two weren't in the military, they were not allowed to come to Grafenwohr and stay with Elvis. During our training in Grafenwohr all the troops had to live and sleep on post.

Elvis' favorite thing to do in Grafenwohr — just about the only thing to do, actually — was going to the Tower Theater on base to watch movies with his buddies. We went almost every night and often saw the same movie three or four nights in a row. We had most of the lines memorized by the fourth night. Elvis had met another GI named Johnny Lange, and the three of us would always go to the movies together.

I noticed this beautiful young woman waiting every night inside the movie lobby, probably trying to sneak a peak of Elvis.

On this particular night, Johnny had gone to the lobby to get us some popcorn and came back saying he spotted the same girl. This time, she had been bold enough to ask Johnny if he would get Elvis' autograph. We didn't know this at the time, but she knew right where we were sitting. When Johnny returned with the popcorn and explained the girl wanted to get an autograph, Elvis sent me back to get her for him.

I found her and gave her the good news.

"Elvis would like to meet you," I said. I could tell from the expression on her face that she couldn't believe this was happening. I walked her down the aisle and sat her right next to Elvis. As fate would have it, this wouldn't be the last time I would take her down the aisle.

The girl's name was Elisabeth Stefaniak, and even though I thought she was extremely attractive, I honestly didn't have any romantic thoughts about her.

Elisabeth was the stepdaughter of career Army Sergeant Raymond McCormick, who was an instructor stationed at Grafenwohr. The dependent housing was on the post where Elisabeth lived with her parents and younger sister, Linda. From the first night Elvis met Elisabeth, he saw her as much as possible. Whenever Elvis had a chance, he would slip away to see Elisabeth.

At first I figured she was just another girl for Elvis to entertain himself with while we were in Grafenwohr. However, a few days after we returned to Friedberg, Elvis called Elisabeth to join us in Bad Nauheim. He was bringing her there as his personal secretary. I could see that she meant a lot more to him than just a secretary by the way he acted so protective of her.

In fact, Elvis warned me and the other guys to stay away from her. He would tell us flat-out his girls were "off limits," and then would keep an eye on the situation and call us on any infractions. Elvis expected the same regarding all girls he dated. But in Elisabeth's case he called a special meeting on the subject. I remember thinking at the time that Elvis would never, ever catch me looking at one of his girls, especially Elisabeth.

CHAPTER EIGHT

Elisabeth's Story

Elisabeth

For most of my young life, I had one foot in two different cultures. I was born Elisabeth Stefaniak on May 27, 1939, in Bamberg, Germany, about 30 miles north of Nuremburg.

From the 10th century onward, this town has been an important link to the Slavic people, especially those of Poland and Pomerania. During its prosperity, from the 12th century onward, the architecture of Bamberg strongly influenced Northern Germany and Hungary. In the late 18th century, it was the center of the Enlightenment in Southern Germany with eminent philosophers such as Hegel and Hoffmann living there. To the Germans, this city is considered the country's best kept secret.

The local Germans said that during the Allied invasion of Germany, toward the end of World War II, Hitler kept his ss troops and other main military regiments away from Bamberg so the city would not be harmed. Only one small bridge in the city was destroyed during the war, leaving the entire city intact without other war damage. In 1973, the city of Bamberg celebrated 1,000 years of existence.

My grandparents, Adam and Kunigunda Grab, my aunt Johanna and her son Robert, had an apartment in the same building where my parents, Georg and Elfriede Stefaniak lived, Gonnerstrasse 40. My widowed Aunt Johanna still lives in that same apartment more than 60 years later. Unlike many Americans, who are quite nomadic, Germans will often live in the same place all their lives.

My mother and father met at a dance in Bamberg in 1938. He was one of the few soldiers stationed at Bamberg at the time. He came from a family of farmers who lived about two hours from Bamberg. I was a direct product of the war.

I was too young to remember my father going off to the Russian front, and for a number of years during the war, my mother did not hear a word from him, other than a report that he was either killed in action, or was a prisoner of war somewhere in Russia.

Toward the end of the war, when I was five, Nuremberg was almost completely destroyed by Allied bombing. Since Bamberg was only 30 miles north of there, the explosions sounded as if they were in our backyard.

War sirens wailed as if they were about to hit us, and we huddled in the dark cellar until the "all clear" alarm sounded. It was a terribly frightening experience for everyone, especially for a young child.

After the war, when the surviving soldiers returned to their hometown of Bamberg, my father was not one of them, so we assumed he was dead. It wasn't until three years later, in 1948, that one night he just showed up unannounced.

My mother and I were so excited to have him back, but that was a fleeting moment. About a week later, the whole ugly truth came out; my father revealed he had married a Russian woman and she bore him a young son. He claimed that he was a prisoner of war in Russia, and she saved his life by getting some guards drunk, and then shooting them. I cannot say whether this incident was true, but it sounded plausible in view of similar war stories we heard.

Since she saved his life, my father felt indebted to her and married her. They lived on a Russian farm until returning to Bamberg. My father had brought his new wife and their son to a refugee camp in Bamberg, and was seriously trying to figure out what to do with his life.

My mother, who had suffered a lifetime of pain over this misfortune, was forced to divorce my father when I was nine years old. I didn't have much of a relationship with my father after that.

I attended a German public school where I spoke in my native language. When I got home from school, my grandmother, Kunigunda, cared for me while my mother worked in the perfume department at the American post exchange (px) at Werner Barracks, Bamberg. Werner Barracks is still an active U.S. Army Post to this day.

Three years after my parents' divorce, my mother met and married Raymond L. McCormick, an Army Sergeant in his early thirties stationed at Bamberg. About 18 months later, when I was 13, my stepfather was reassigned to duty in the States.

The move was fairly traumatic for me. I had just started taking horseback riding lessons and had major reservations about leaving my grandmother, my aunt, and my cousin, Robert. I was especially close to my grandmother. Often when I was little, she would put me on the back of her bicycle and off we'd go for an adventure in the city to go shopping or out to the country to visit relatives. She was my best friend and I loved her very much. When the time came to leave, it was hard to say goodbye to the only life I knew.

We came to the United States by ship in November, 1953. Along with other GI's and families, we took an Army ship called *Upshur* to the States. It was not the *Queen Elizabeth*.

I was seasick before the ship even left port, and it worsened when we began our voyage. I was nauseated the entire time and became deathly ill from dehydration. I could only stomach soda crackers and Coca-Cola. The ship finally docked in New York City after 12 grueling days at sea.

Like many foreigners who came to the U.S., the Statue of Liberty was the first landmark I saw when we entered the harbor of New York City.

Right away, we went to a drugstore and my mother ordered ice cream for us. When the waitress brought us our bowls of ice cream, she also brought each of us a glass of water. My mother and I thought it was such a strange American custom. Even to this day, you don't get water with a meal in a German restaurant unless you ask for it, and you still won't get it with ice. Even German beer is consumed at room temperature. Germans have convinced themselves that a cold drink is bad for your stomach.

Soon we were on our way to Baltimore, Maryland, which was about a three-hour drive. My stepfather, who asked us to call him "Mac," was being stationed at the Aberdeen, Maryland, Proving Grounds, U.S. Army Base near Baltimore.

After we got settled in and I started school, I worried about the language barrier. I should have been attending eighth grade, but because of my limited English, school officials recommended that I start in the first grade.

"I will not be going to any school if I have to start over in the first grade," I yelled at my mother. "I want to be with kids my own age."

In Germany, I did well both academically and socially. Finally, the school administration relented and agreed to let me try and immerse myself for one year to see if my English would improve.

I remember one incident my first year when my classmates were electing student body officers. I didn't understand what was happening because we didn't do that in Germany. When the word "president" was mentioned, I assumed President Eisenhower was coming to my school. I was often confused, which was frustrating and at times isolating. Looking back on that period of my life, I realize I was shy and emotionally fragile.

I was, however, blessed with a wonderful teacher, Ms. Lauderbach, who came to my house twice a week to teach me English. She came on her own time and would never accept any money. Within a year's time, I learned the basics; and after three years, I could speak and write English well enough for everyone to understand me.

Over time, I grew to love the United States and became a typical American teenager. Like all girls at that time, I fell in love with Elvis Presley. The first time I saw him was on *The Ed Sullivan Show* in 1956. No doubt about it, he was different from anyone I had ever seen before, and I liked his style. The moves, the singing, and his attitude made a winning combination. Even my mother liked him, though my stepfather wasn't too crazy about him. I don't think too many fathers back in 1956 were terribly taken with Elvis.

I collected all of his records and bought all the fan magazines. All the girls talked about him at school and I was included in their conversations but Elvis Presley was more than just a teenage idol to me. He helped me bridge the cultural barrier with my American counterparts. I was just getting comfortable with my surroundings when, in my senior year, my stepfather got orders to go back to Germany.

Since I had my family back in Germany, the move wasn't as traumatic as the first, but again, I felt as though I didn't fit in. Even though I was born in Germany, now I felt like an American at heart. Germans considered me an American, while Americans viewed me as a German.

I finished my senior year at Nuremburg American High School. Shortly thereafter, my stepfather was transferred to the U.S. Army training base at Grafenwohr to teach ammunition classes. Since I was not a German citizen, I could not work in Germany. The Army post only hired Germans.

Grafenwohr was a very remote place to live, with not much activity going on for a teenager. The only thing I could do was help my mother with housework and take care of my sister, Linda McCormick, who was five years old.

I was a 19-year-old young lady living in an area with 50,000 GI's, and my stepfather wouldn't let me look at any one of them. He spent too much time with them and knew what was on their minds. I was, however, keeping tabs on Elvis' whereabouts in Germany through *Bravo* magazine and *Stars and Stripes*. Then one day, I finally realized the advantage of living in Grafenwohr.

I read in *Stars and Stripes* that Elvis Presley would be training in Grafenwohr for three weeks. Eventually, every American GI in West Germany was required to receive their training in Grafenwohr. It was the main training center for all U.S. Army troops stationed in West Germany.

I was determined to meet my idol. Within 24 hours, everyone was talking about Elvis. You can imagine how excited I was, a huge fan who had collected his records and watched every one of his television appearances and all of his movies.

This was the perfect opportunity to see him and get his autograph. It would be my dream come true.

I had heard Elvis was seen going to the Tower Theater on post, so I made a beeline for it. I didn't notice Elvis, but it was hard to determine by looking at the backs of 500 GI's. I had been to the theater enough times that I was friendly with the manager. He was kind enough to confirm that Elvis and a couple of his GI buddies had been to the theater, and they usually arrived about 10 minutes after the movie started, and left 10 minutes early.

The next night I went to the theater well before the movie, *The Young Lions* starring Marlon Brando, began playing. I stood in the lobby watching every GI as they came into the theater. Once the movie started they would cut the lights. I knew that if I were to see him, it would have to be before the movie started. I waited and waited, but no Elvis.

Finally, in desperation I asked the manager if Elvis and his buddies had come tonight, and much to my delight, he told me they had.

"He walked right past you and you didn't know it," the manager informed me. All of the soldiers looked alike in uniform, but I couldn't believe I didn't recognize Elvis.

Next, the manager did me a huge favor and pointed out the approximate location where Elvis was seated. So there I was, standing in the back of a dark movie theater trying to get a glimpse of Elvis, and all I saw was an endless sea of crewcuts. I didn't have the nerve to walk down that aisle and look for Elvis, but I did not take my eyes off the area the manager pointed out. I stood in the same spot for what seemed liked hours trying to pick him out of the crowd. I was just about to give up when I noticed a GI getting up from where the manager had told me. I observed it wasn't Elvis as he passed by me to go to the concession stand.

On his way back, I mustered up the courage to approach him. "Excuse me, mister, would you happen to be sitting with Elvis Presley?" I asked.

He nodded yes, and said that he was sitting in the seat right next to him. He also mentioned he was a good buddy to Elvis. I couldn't believe what I was hearing. I was so nervous that I could barely hand this GI my piece of paper for Elvis' autograph. Later I found out his name was Johnny Lange. Johnny told me he would be glad to ask Elvis for the autograph. I watched Johnny go back to his seat with the popcorn. After a few minutes a different GI got up from beside Elvis and walked up the aisle towards me.

"Elvis wants you to come down and sit with him," the GI said to me.

I thought I was going to faint. All I wanted was his autograph, and now I was invited to join him. Not even in my wildest dreams did I ever imagine this would happen. I was shaking from excitement and had butterflies in my stomach that wouldn't settle down. The poor GI walking me down the aisle had to keep me from falling because I was so nervous.

When we arrived where Elvis was sitting, this GI sat me down right next to Elvis, and then he sat down beside me. I had no way of knowing this wouldn't be the last time this GI would take me down the aisle.

His name was Rex Mansfield. I was so wrapped up in meeting Elvis, I didn't even remember that it was Rex who walked me down the aisle. Rex completely understood that, of course, because I was very infatuated with Elvis.

The first close-up look I had of Elvis was the most fantastic feeling I had experienced in all of my 19 years. I thought he was the most handsome, most beautiful hunk of man I had ever seen.

"What's your name, darlin'?" he asked in that Southern drawl as he put his arm around me. I cannot remember anything I said to him. All I did was look blurry-eyed and mumbled something. Here I was, sitting with the most famous GI in the world as he held my hand and whispered sweet things in my ear. Needless to say, I was floating on cloud nine.

We all ended up exiting the theater shortly before the movie ended. Elvis told his two buddies he would see them later and walked me home, which was about 10 minutes away.

On the way home that first night we talked about the Army, what I was doing in Grafenwohr, and about my family. Elvis was genuinely interested in what I had to say and listened to every word. We were standing by a tree, in the courtyard of my parents' apartment, when he surprised me with a good night kiss.

I was still nervous, and wasn't sure what to say or do next.

"Would you like to come in and meet my parents?" I asked him. He promised to meet them some other time. When he left me at the door, I was almost paralyzed. We promised to meet the following night at the theater.

I told my parents about my experience with Elvis the second I shut the door. Initially, they thought I was making the whole story up. Finally I convinced them it was the truth. My mother was excited, and also a bit disappointed that she didn't get the chance to meet him.

My stepfather, Mac, didn't think it was such a big deal. In fact, Mac, like most older Americans, thought Elvis was nothing more than a bum and a bad influence on our younger generation.

I did not sleep one wink all that night as I relived every moment in my head. I was hoping for an autograph, and instead,

I ended up with a date. To top it off, he was a perfect gentleman with impeccable manners. That night, November 20, 1958, will be forever etched in my mind. For the next six nights, I met Elvis at the theater and then he would walk me home.

On Thanksgiving Day, November 27, he showed up unannounced at my doorstep, ready to meet my parents. I think he came that day because he missed his family. This would be his first Thanksgiving ever without his beloved mother, Gladys. Unfortunately, it wasn't the welcome he expected.

When my mother and I arrived home, we noticed about 25 kids standing at the entrance to our building. When we asked the kids what all the commotion was, we learned that Elvis had arrived about 15 minutes earlier in a taxi and was upstairs in our neighbor's apartment.

Later I found out what really happened. Elvis rang our doorbell and my five-year-old sister, Linda answered. The man standing there said hello and introduced himself. Since the name Elvis Presley meant nothing to her, she would not let him in. He asked to see me and Linda told him I was gone somewhere with our mother. Little sister Linda finally told Elvis her father was sleeping and she would have to check with him, leaving Elvis standing at the door. When my sister woke daddy, he didn't believe her story and went back to sleep. The neighbor across the hall overheard the misadventure, and let Elvis in his apartment.

During that first visit to our place he told us about his family, and spoke fondly about his mother who had died only a little over three months before. I could see how much Elvis loved and adored his mother by the way he described how special she was and how much he missed her. He painfully mentioned that his dad was already dating other women, which brought tears to his eyes.

Elvis asked us about German customs, and we gave him a quick lesson in our culture. We talked about how the Germans love their beer and how the man of the house was always served first at every meal. Then the subject switched to why there was no speed limit on the autobahn.

"Why is it so darned cold here all the time?" Elvis asked. He was told that it was easier to understand if you considered the fact that central Germany would be in the same position as 100 miles north of the Canadian border on the world map. I was thrilled the entire evening and my parents were very impressed with his manners. Elvis was a perfect gentleman and would say "yes ma'am" or "yes sir" to everything.

Elvis expressed a genuine interest in my stepfather's army career, which boosted Mac's ego and helped create a bond between them. After becoming acquainted with him that Thanksgiving Day, Mac became extremely fond of Elvis.

We borrowed a guitar from a neighbor and Elvis became the evening's entertainment. He sang mostly Marty Robbins tunes, saying he loved his Gunfighter Ballads. Rarely did Elvis ever sing any of his own songs and we never sang along because no one in my family could carry a tune.

After that Thanksgiving night, Elvis became a regular fixture at our house. He arrived daily, always at unexpected times. Sometimes he would show up in the morning for his special breakfast food. He would go in the kitchen and explain to my mother how he would like to have his eggs and bacon cooked. He was so sweet and polite, muttie (German for mom) would have fixed him anything he wanted.

He would come back in the early evening and take me to the movie showing, or just sit around and talk with me and my family.

Elvis felt comfortable, like he was part of our family. My family would usually go to bed early on purpose, so Elvis and I could have some privacy. This was a very special time for me to get to know and understand him better.

Elvis was also close to his family. He would call home to his Bad Nauheim residence. Most of the time Red West or Lamar Fike would answer, and then he would ask them to call back so as to not use our phone for long distance calls. His father, Vernon Presley, would usually phone him right back if he was there when Elvis called. He mostly called to check up on Vernon and his grandma. I could overhear him telling his dad about meeting this "very nice girl in Grafenwohr," and he was spending a lot of time with her and her family. I was flattered that he liked me so much that he chose to tell his father about me. It was still hard for me to believe I was dating Elvis Presley.

Elvis usually came over to our house by taxi. On a few occasions he showed up driving an Army jeep. When my stepfather had to go on a three-day field trip, he offered Elvis use of our family car. Neither my mother nor I had a German driver's license. Having a car allowed Elvis more flexibility with his visits, and he came more often.

The word had gotten out that Elvis and I were an item. It became obvious to us that the neighbors from our housing area were keeping an eye on our place. As soon as they noticed Elvis' arrival, they would run out of their building and line up in front of our apartment waiting for autographs and photos. I think the family that lived directly across the hall from our fourth floor apartment was actually watching for Elvis through their peep-hole. Seconds after Elvis rang our doorbell and entered the apartment, they were ringing our doorbell. After awhile, it was hard to believe these were mere coincidences. This pushy couple would bring over their two small children and a guitar so Elvis could entertain them. They wouldn't let him rest, and if they weren't requesting music, they were asking question after question. This intrusion on our privacy became quite annoying to Elvis and my family.

After a few evenings, Elvis figured out how to come in through the back door of our basement and sneak up the stairwell to our apartment. When he visited at night, he would not turn on the stairwell lights, so the nosy neighbors could not see who was at our door.

Around this time the Hula Hoop was a big fad, and my little sister was really good at it. She wanted Elvis to try it, but Elvis, who could swing his hips better than anyone in the world, could not master the Hula Hoop. If I had not seen it with my own eyes, I would have never believed it.

When he wasn't humoring my sister, he napped on our living room couch in the middle of the morning or afternoon. In the evenings, we went to the movie house or just drove around. Elvis told me about his daily life which included training, target prac-tice, and the freezing weather conditions in which he had to perform these tasks. He also explained how the media worked, and warned me they would exaggerate his exploits to the point of extreme. I was glad he addressed that issue. In the past, I had always assumed what I read in print was the truth. Of course, we could never go out in public and this suited me fine because that way I didn't have to share him with anybody.

Toward the end of his training in Grafenwohr, Elvis went to the PX and bought my parents a beautiful 365-day gold clock and brought it to the apartment. It was his way of thanking my parents for all their hospitality. He and my stepfather sat on the floor and spent hours assembling it. When they finally got the clock put together, it would not work. Elvis took it back to the PX the very next day and exchanged it for one that worked. The last night Elvis spent in Grafenwohr before going back to the Friedberg Kaserne, something happened that changed my life forever.

Elvis told my parents about all the fan mail he had and how desperately he needed a secretary: one who could speak, read, and write both German and English to assist with these letters.

"Elisabeth is perfect for the job. She would stay in her own private room at the Hotel Grunewald in Bad Nauheim," he said. "I assure you that she will be in good hands with me and my father and grandmother, and we will take full responsibility for her." Considering everything that had happened over the course of two weeks, this was the most inconceivable of all.

"You think about it. You don't have to give me an answer now, darlin'. I will call for you in a couple of days," Elvis said to me as he was leaving. When he said good night and bid farewell, I honestly thought that was the last time I would see Elvis, but I prayed it wouldn't be.

My parents didn't have to think about it very long before they agreed to let me go with Elvis, although I believe I would have gone with or without their blessing. Nobody was going to stop me from living in Elvis Presley's residence.

This was a once-in-a-lifetime offer I wasn't going to pass up.

CHAPTER NINE
Good Job in
Bad Nauheim

Elisabeth

Three days after Elvis left me at Grafenwohr, he called to ask how fast I could come to Bad Nauheim. He mentioned there were about 50 duffel bags full of fan mail waiting to be sorted out, and one-third of the mail was from German fans. "The sooner the better, darlin'," Elvis advised in his own special way.

He told me to discuss this situation with my parents and call him soon with an answer. I was ready to go right then and there, but after talking it over with my parents, I called him back with a date. "I can be there in one week," I told him, which made him very happy. I got there the first part of December.

I'll never forget that train ride. I was so excited and nervous it seemed to take forever to reach Bad Nauheim. I hadn't been away from my parents for any great length of time, so this was a big show of independence. I even had to change trains at the big Frankfurt Bahnhof station. It was the longest trip I had ever taken by myself and I had no idea what to expect once I got there. I intended to stay as long as Elvis was in Germany, so I packed

93

almost all the clothes I owned. Five hours later, my two large suitcases and I arrived in Bad Nauheim.

Elvis explained that he would be on duty when my train arrived, but he would send his father Vernon to meet me. We had previously arranged a signal since his father didn't know what I looked like. I said I would be wearing a red coat, which would make it easy to identify me.

I was greeted by Vernon Presley, Lamar Fike, and Red West. Lamar and Red said they were civilian buddies of Elvis and had been his bodyguards and companions in Memphis before Elvis was drafted into the Army.

We drove directly to the Hotel Grunewald where the group was residing at the time. Elvis had rented the entire top floor at the hotel to accommodate his friends and family.

Vernon showed me to my room, which doubled as an office. It was on the floor just below them. It was a big corner room about twice the size of a normal hotel room. It was a good thing it was such a large room since half of it was occupied with duffel bags filled with fan mail.

Then I met Minnie Mae Presley — Vernon's mother and Elvis' grandmother. She was preparing an authentic Southern meal for everyone, but it was really for the benefit of Elvis, who liked his food cooked a certain way.

The kitchen in the hotel was very small with a big dining table in the center. There was no shortage of food on the table. The four men seated around it had large appetites and had no trouble putting away the generous amounts of food.

Minnie Mae was a tall, slender lady with a great sense of humor. I think she was really glad to have some female companionship; she smiled constantly as we talked. We hit it off that night and I knew we would be great friends. She accepted me right away like one of the family.

"Elvis told me that he was bringing a real sweet girl into the group to help out," Minnie Mae said. "I'm glad to know it's going to be you." She asked me to call her "Grandma" instead of Mrs. Presley, and I was only too happy to oblige. I was the answer to her prayers as she now had someone else to help her care for Elvis and the boys.

The first thing Elvis did when he arrived from the Friedberg Kaserne was give me a big hug and kiss. "Foghorn, you don't know how darn glad I am to see you," Elvis said, swooping me up off my feet. He nicknamed me Foghorn because of my low voice in the morning.

I noticed that Elvis joked and clowned around during dinner, which surprised me because I had not seen that side of Elvis before. He was relaxed and really let his guard down around his family and companions.

Lamar and Red asked me some questions about myself, but I could tell Elvis had already told them some things concerning my upbringing. They expressed how grateful they were to have help with the fan mail, especially the German mail, because it was getting out of hand.

"Foghorn, the boys are going to show you how I like the mail to be answered," Elvis assured me.

After dinner I helped Grandma clean in the kitchen and then joined the gang in the living room. We all sat around and became better acquainted with each other. Being homesick wasn't even an option, because it never occurred to me. This place instantly felt like home.

I was so curious about the fan mail that I couldn't wait until morning. I stayed up the entire night reading letters. A majority of the people requested autographed pictures. Some of the letters had Christian medals inside for Elvis, and other letters asked for financial assistance. There was also an abundance of love letters, and a fraction of hate letters from jealous boyfriends or husbands. Some fans wrote notes to Elvis to let him know how much they loved and enjoyed his music.

One letter writer in particular sticks out in my mind even to this day. Everyday Elvis received a love letter and baked cookies from a love-starved woman from Indiana. Every letter described her dreams in detail, which always consisted of romantic evenings with Elvis.

"Thank you, my darling, for coming to see me last night and for the wonderful time we had together," her letter read.

Some of the things she wrote I cannot put on paper. In her fantasy world, Elvis was madly in love with her and they were conducting a torrid love affair. She sent photos of herself, which revealed an unattractive woman in her mid-fifties. Elvis never ate any of her cookies, nor the baked goods that others sent, for fear of poisoning. We threw away tons of delicious looking food, but better to be safe than sorry.

Most fans sent a postcard-type picture of Elvis they wanted autographed, plus a self-addressed stamped envelope. There was a hand stamp made of Elvis' signature. For the pictures I could use the stamp autograph. If they sent a plain sheet of paper asking for his signature, the stamp couldn't be used. It would look too obvious that it was a stamp, so in these cases I would sign the plain sheets of paper with Elvis' signature. The guys could copy Elvis' signature almost exactly and, eventually, so could I. It was no easy feat – I practiced many hours learning to duplicate his signature.

We were provided with autographed pictures of Elvis that we would send with each postcard or letter. Vernon purchased the German stamps which cost about $500 a month.

Some of the letters were written in other European languages, but most were from Germany. I handled very little fan mail from the States as Colonel Parker had someone else handling nearly all of that mail.

The American mail was organized in special bags and mailed to Colonel Parker. Usually we waited until there were 20 or more bags, and Vernon would employ Lamar and Red to help him carry them to the post office. All military personnel stationed overseas were entitled to use an Army Post Office (APO) number so the cost of the mail was the same as if mailed in the U.S. As they dropped off mail to send to Colonel Parker, they would pick up new mail that awaited them at the German Post Office.

While Elvis was pulling his daily duty at the Friedberg Kaserne, Lamar and Red helped me answer the fan mail. Elvis never got involved with the details of my job. It was Vernon who really took charge, and I would go to him for questions or concerns, although Lamar and Red always were helpful and easy to approach.

I usually started my workday around 8 a.m. and worked until Elvis came home for lunch, usually between 11:45 a.m. and 12:45 p.m. Many times I helped Grandma clean up the kitchen after we ate lunch. I started to work with the mail again around 1:30 p.m. This was the routine almost every day.

I also learned that the Presleys, especially Elvis, had nicknames for nearly everyone. "E" was for Elvis. Bill Norvell was named "Nervous Norvell" by Elvis because he always acted like he was nervous. Rex became "Rexadus" which had no meaning at all, except as a term of endearment and because Elvis liked the sound of the name. Vernon called Elvis "Son," "Sonny," or "Sonny Boy." Grandma called Red "Fire Eyes," and Lamar was also known as "Belly" or "Buddha." Grandma was called "Dodger" or "Miss Minnie."

The name Dodger was acquired by Grandma back when Elvis was a young boy. In the midst of a temper tantrum he threw a baseball, just missing Grandma's head. Elvis always explained she earned the name because "she dodged out of the way so fast."

Most of the evenings were spent just casually sitting around, chatting, joking, and playing records but whatever we did usually centered on Elvis. Rex would often visit, and Lamar and Red each brought girlfriends over. Elvis loved to have fun, and sometimes he would sing parodies to one of his hit songs. Elvis' hotel suite was even equipped with a piano.

He used to listen to Roy Hamilton's greatest hits album, and liked to make fun of a song called "Don't Let Go." Elvis discovered toward the end of the song that the lyrics became inaudible then the song finished with the words, "Hound dog barking upside the hill." Elvis played that particular part over and over, shaking his head at the apparent nonsense of it. "The hound dog barking upside the hill has nothing to do with the other lyrics, and the song makes absolutely no sense," he often said with a mystifying smile, amusing himself.

On the other hand, Elvis loved Hamilton's version of "I Believe" and "You'll Never Walk Alone." He would play the songs by ear on the piano and have Rex, Red, Lamar, and Charlie sing along with him. Rex had a high tenor voice, and Elvis continued raising the keys higher on the piano until Rex's voice cracked. This would send them all into laughing fits. Elvis was not making fun of Rex's voice — he was actually impressed because his voice was so high.

Another group he enjoyed listening to was the Harmonizing Four, a black gospel group from Richmond, Virginia. His favorite song of theirs was "Farther Along." The bass singer had such a low voice that Elvis was astonished by it, and try as he might, he could not come close to duplicating it. He showed us on the piano that the lowest note in this song was actually off the keyboard. He also favored two other songs by the Harmonizing Four called "All Things Are Possible" and "When I've Done the Best I Can." Another group special to Elvis was the Statesman Gospel Quartet from Memphis, because he knew each member of the quartet personally.

Elvis' love of music often drew the ire of the guests on the floor below us. They did not appreciate the loud singing, guitar playing, and rowdy behavior of Elvis' entourage. On top of that there was the nuisance of his fans who constantly hung around outside, hoping to spot Elvis when he came home for lunch and after work. The other tenants of the hotel constantly complained to the manager, and we were finally ordered to move.

Personally, I had more worries on my mind than just the move. Shortly after I arrived in Bad Nauheim, the bomb dropped. No, not an atomic bomb, but it might as well have been, aimed right at my heart.

"Foghorn, a girl named Janie Wilbanks will be staying with us during Christmas and I want you to make her feel at home when she comes to town," Elvis told me firmly but politely. Janie had made headlines in all the papers and magazines when Elvis came through Memphis by train on his way to Germany. As if her coming wasn't bad enough, Elvis also informed me that Janie would be sharing my office/bedroom for a few weeks.

I became instantly jealous and resented the fact that she was coming. In Grafenwohr, there was no competition and I had Elvis all to myself. I had seen a picture of Janie from the newspapers and knew she was a beautiful girl. Then again, Elvis didn't date ugly women, and I must say, he had great taste in beauty.

But as I got to know Janie, I couldn't help but like her. She was very sweet and instantly fell in love with Grandma. Also, she pitched in with the kitchen chores and helped me with the fan mail. As far as Janie was concerned, I was Elvis' secretary. I never confided to her my true feelings for Elvis, nor the exact nature of my relationship with him.

That first Christmas in 1958 at the Grunewald Hotel was an extremely depressing time for Elvis, Vernon, and Grandma. This was their first Christmas without Gladys. This was also a difficult and dark period for the Germans. Most of the country, including the municipality of Bad Nauheim, was still struggling to get over the financial impact of World War II. Even the Grunewald Hotel downplayed the Christmas holiday. It was a low-key affair and Christmas was just another day for the Presley family.

As Janie made more visits to the house, she and I became very close friends, and shared some good times together. We cooked in the kitchen, or sat in Grandma's bedroom for hours talking and laughing. Grandma would tell us about her relatives from Mississippi. Janie was also from Mississippi and could relate to all these stories.

Our friendship really surprised me — after all, she was my chief competition for the time being. I think Janie and I realized we were just two of many girls vying for Elvis' attention, and accepting that fact of life brought us much closer. Janie was the first of many more to come. Beautiful girls were constantly coming and going out of the hotel. I had to painfully accept this, and just grin and bear it.

Elvis had his own taxi driver, Joseph Wehrheim, who also served both as a chauffeur and errand boy. One of his regular errands was to go to Frankfurt every two weeks to pick up Margit Buergin. After a few dates with Elvis back in Grafenwohr, he had explained to me that his relationship with Margit was exaggerated by the media.

"Darlin', the press has blown my friendship with Margit way out of proportion. That's the way the press works," Elvis said. He had met the 16-year-old German girl at a park in Bad Homburg. She was a student and worked as a typist for an electrical supply company. After Margit appeared in photographs with Elvis she became an overnight sensation. "Elvis is a very nice boy and I like him very much," she was quoted as saying by the press. She received at least 40 letters a day and had many requests for interviews.

Margit would spend the evening at the Hotel Grunewald with Elvis. They weren't comparing philosophies of life, because she hardly spoke any English. Eventually I became the translator between Elvis and Margit. Whenever Elvis attempted to tell her something, she smiled at him, then turned to me and said she didn't understand.

"Foghorn, tell her what I said in German," Elvis directed. Sometimes Margit talked with me more than she did with Elvis. It was an awkward position Elvis had put me in. He was the man I adored, and the last thing I was interested in was helping their relationship blossom. A few times I was tempted to tell Margit that Elvis said he wanted to call the whole thing off and don't ever come back. But in the end I didn't have to, because she did herself in. The romance between them fizzled after Margit posed for pictures in the American soldier's magazine, *Overseas Weekly*. The spread featured several pictures of Margit and an article declaring that she was Elvis' German fräulein. Auf wiedersehen, Margit!

I often wondered how Anita Wood, Elvis' girlfriend back in Memphis, must have felt when she read in the American press about his alleged love affair with Margit. How would Elvis explain it to her? Better yet, what would I say to Anita when the word got out that I was living with the Presleys?

Elvis wasn't the only one looking for love in Germany. Lamar took Elvis' lead and fell in love with a local girl. I enjoyed listening to him talk about her when she wasn't around. It was evident to everyone except Lamar that his girlfriend was just using him to get close to Elvis. Whenever she came around, she flirted outrageously with Elvis. They say love is blind, and in this particular case, Lamar was not only blind, but deaf and dumb, too!

While Lamar spent most of his free time with his girl, Red mostly occupied his time at Beck's Bar getting into fights. If ever anyone liked fighting, it was Red West. Many guys liked to pick on Red since they knew he was Elvis' bodyguard, but they got more than they bargained for when they matched fists with him. Red was absolutely fearless and never lost a fight as far as I can recall. Not all of Red's bouts were Elvis-related. Red was accustomed to signing bar tabs in the States, but that didn't work in Germany. The owners weren't impressed that he was a friend of Elvis', and he was expected to pay in Deutsch Marks like everyone else.

One night I had a surprise visit from Red. I was almost asleep when I heard someone knocking on my door. I invited him in, and he sat on the floor near my bed. I could tell he had been out drinking. He was in a relationship with a girl named Kathy and wanted to confide in me. They were having some problems. Although I didn't mind the company, it was difficult to concentrate on what

Red was saying, and all I could do was pray that Elvis didn't unexpectedly come by. Red and I both knew the rules. Red's presence in my room made me nervous. I sighed in relief when Red finished talking about Kathy and went to his own room. If Elvis had walked in on us, I would have been on the next train to Grafenwohr and Red would have been shipped back home to Memphis.

Red wasn't quite as worried as me. He was a daredevil, and I don't think he cared as much as I did how Elvis would react. Elvis had a lot of respect for Red, and in return Red got away with more than anyone. Also, I think Elvis had a bit of fear of Red's temper. Later on, Kathy stayed with us when we moved, and helped me for a couple of months with the ever-growing fan mail.

I was genuinely fond of Red and Lamar, and we got along great. I had become just like a sister to them. The two would often come to me on Fridays to borrow money. They usually hit me up for a couple of marks apiece since Elvis didn't pay them a salary. Elvis had them on a short leash and they were forced to ask either me or Vernon for cash, and Vernon was not exactly known for his generosity with money. At most, Vernon gave them a couple of marks apiece, which barely paid for a beer.

Rarely did the two men ever pay back loans from me, but it didn't bother me much. They also asked me for advice about the girls they dated. Unfortunately, they couldn't give me any advice on how to keep Elvis' attention solely on me.

I eventually learned the hard way that there wasn't an answer to that problem, because no one woman could hold Elvis Presley's attention for very long.

CHAPTER TEN

A Home Away From Home

Elisabeth

In February 1959, Vernon Presley found a three-story, six-bedroom fully furnished white stucco house at Goethestrasse 14 in Bad Nauheim.

The house came equipped with one huge bathroom upstairs which everyone in the house used; a half bathroom downstairs, a glassed-in porch off the kitchen, a large living room, and an unfinished basement for storage. Best of all was the location, which was about 10 blocks from the Hotel Grunewald.

The monthly rent was 3,000 German marks, or a little more than $700 a month, which was about 10 times what it was worth at that time. The landlord, Frau Pieper, knew it was Elvis Presley renting the house and conveniently added the "movie star tax" to hike up the tab. Nevertheless, Elvis was excited to have a place to call home and quickly moved in.

When Elvis struck the deal with Frau Pieper, part of the agreement was that she could stay in the home and keep her own bedroom, which was downstairs right next to the living room. In Germany, many of the older houses were built without a den, and the living room was where everyone gathered. This was the case at Goethestrasse 14, which made things more than a little inconvenient for Frau Pieper. She constantly complained that the noise kept her from sleeping.

"We warned you about this, but you insisted on staying in this bedroom," I reminded her. Elvis and Vernon said they didn't care about her inconvenience, since it was her choice to stay. We even offered to rent out a small place for her temporarily, but she wouldn't budge. She was a controlling old lady who wanted to keep an eye on her place.

Another annoyance Frau Pieper posed was that she did not understand a word of English. That made me the only person in the house able to communicate with her. Frau Pieper couldn't pass by Elvis without giving him a great, big bear hug, which he could have done without. But he would smile at her as if he didn't mind, all the while muttering such endearments as, "Get away from me you fat slob." That was actually one of the kinder names he called her. Since she didn't comprehend English, she was none the wiser. When Frau Pieper asked me what Elvis had said, I would cover for him.

"He said you look nice today," I'd say, or tell her that Elvis had complimented her lovely smile.

Later I would tell Elvis what I had said, and we would all have a good laugh at Frau Pieper's expense. It was also amusing to watch Grandma and Frau Pieper in the kitchen cooking and trying to get along with each other. Frau Pieper loved to talk, even though Grandma didn't understand a word she said. As Grandma fixed her American dishes, Frau Pieper watched and asked me many questions.

"I wish you'd just stay out of my kitchen," Grandma would say rather bluntly. It didn't matter, of course, since the Frau was clueless, except for the time when Grandma got so fed up with Frau Pieper that she chased her out of her own kitchen with a broom.

The kitchen conflicts were almost nothing next to the bathroom war. There was just one place to bathe, in the upstairs bathroom. It was challenging to say the least, living with six people and only one bathtub.

Elvis rented a piano for $40 a month to put in the living room. I was amazed at how well he could play by ear. He could not read a word of music, but he sure could play the heck out of that piano. We all enjoyed listening to him play, feeling as though we were part of something very special — having our own private Elvis concert!

It wasn't long after we moved in that a picture of our new residence was published in all the local magazines and newspapers. Once again, hundreds of fans started showing up outside the doors. But Elvis didn't seem to mind. He was always appreciative of his fans and never took them for granted.

Grandma cooked all the meals since Elvis preferred her cooking and always liked the same menu. Every weekday morning we woke up at 4:30 a.m., and by 5:00 breakfast was ready. I often helped Grandma cook, because it was always a large meal. It usually consisted of slightly burned bacon, hard fried eggs, peaches, homemade Southern baked biscuits with butter, jam, and coffee. Grandma cooked the food in accordance with Elvis' taste, even though some of us would have preferred scrambled eggs and bacon that was not cremated. We ate the meals the way Elvis wanted them prepared, or we ate nothing.

Elvis left the house by 5:30 to report to the Friedberg Kaserne. Right after he left, we all went back to sleep for a couple more hours. Since there was nothing else for Red and Lamar to do, they often slept until 11 o'clock. They woke up and got dressed just as Elvis arrived home for lunch. This infuriated Frau Pieper because she liked to make the beds and clean the house early. Another part of the agreement that allowed Frau Pieper to remain in the house was that she served as Presley's "Dienstmadchen," which is German for "the maid." But Frau Pieper was no "maid to order," that's for sure!

Elvis arrived at the house for lunch at 11:45, unless he was in the field training or on maneuvers. When Elvis drove the car around the corner about a block away on Goethestrasse, he would take quick inventory of the situation in front of the house. Sometimes there were only a dozen people waiting for him. In this case, he would park at the front of the house and sign autographs for about 15 minutes before coming in for lunch. If the waiting crowd was unusually large, he would stop the car where he was and slowly back up out of sight. Then he would park on a side street and jump over the hedge rows and fences and come in the back door through my office.

Occasionally, a fan figured out that Elvis was entering the house through a back way, and tried to do the same. On more than one occasion, I'd catch someone peering through the glass window of my office. This frightened me, so I would go to the back door and talk to them.

"If you want to see Elvis, please go to the front of the house," I said in a stern voice. I never had any problems, as the fans were usually well behaved.

Like breakfast, the menu rarely varied when it came to serving lunch. It was usually sauerkraut and wieners, Hormel chili without beans, Crowder peas or what I called a "goofy sandwich" made by Grandma. This strange sandwich was made of peeled and sliced potatoes fried in grease with "burnt" bacon. Each slice of American bread had mustard and slices of raw onions. I can only imagine the fat and calories in this greasy concoction.

Elvis normally came home around 5:15 p.m., and dinner was ready by 6 p.m. On the occasions Red and Lamar picked up pizza, we were in heaven. At Elvis' request, Grandma fixed the special peanut butter and banana toasted sandwich for his dinner. That appealed to us about as much as the goofy sandwich. In the evening, Elvis signed autographs longer and spent more time visiting and talking with the fans. There was even a sign posted on the front of the house that read AUTOGRAPHS BETWEEN 7:30 and 8:30 p.m.

On weekends, Charlie Hodge would come over from Butzbach, another U.S. Army Kaserne, where he was stationed. Charlie was a seasoned guitar player, and he would sing with Rex. Since there was no extra bed for Charlie, he slept on the couch, which also went in the book of demerits kept by Frau Pieper.

Rex and Charlie were two of the closest friends that Elvis had from the Army. There were plenty of other GI's who came around on a regular basis, but it was obvious that Rex and Charlie were his favorites, just as I became Grandma's favorite.

In addition to helping her clean up after meals, sometimes I would help with the cooking. In addition, I had my office work as a secretary, and this was the only job I was paid to do. Vernon paid me a salary of $35 a week in cash on Fridays, and of course I got free room and board. I was rich compared to Red and Lamar. Their room and board was also free, but their pay was the privilege of being in Germany with Elvis. They had too much pride to ask Elvis for money, so he didn't give them any.

I was raised to respect my elders, so helping Grandma was an instinctive thing for me. She was in her seventies and always appreciated it when I assisted her. In fact, we had fun together while we cooked and cleaned. I never thought twice about the many extra working hours I spent helping her.

Grandma worshipped her grandson, but his fame didn't affect her in the least bit. She didn't want or need anything but the roof over her head. There was a lot of cooking to do for the six of us, but it seemed she relished every minute of it. She was a good Southern cook and taught me how to make some of her specialties. When she got sick or went to bed, I took over and did the cooking.

In time, Grandma and I became more or less dependent on each other for companionship. We spent hours talking in her bedroom at night, just girl-talk stuff. Occasionally, I would help her write letters to her daughters in the States. She told me about when Elvis was a little boy. Grandma explained to me how his mother Gladys was extremely protective of him, and how she walked him to school everyday to make sure he arrived safely. When he got older and entered high school, she would continue the habit, but walk a block or so behind to keep from embarrassing him. If another child started a fight with young Elvis, Gladys would quickly come to his aid and even finish his battles for him.

"She beat the tar out of a few of them," Grandma laughed, admiring Gladys' spunk and her willingness to put up her dukes for her boy.

Gladys might have been a bit extreme, but Grandma had a few quirks of her own. I discovered she never took a bath. The tub in Elvis' bathroom was too deep, and at her age she was afraid that if she got in she'd need help getting out. However, there was a sink and mirror in her bedroom. She washed herself every day with a washcloth from head to toe. Then she dried herself off with a bath towel. She never had any body odor and always looked neat in her

Southern country-style dresses. She always wore dresses, and did not own any pants.

The ladylike effect of the dresses was somewhat offset by the toothpick constantly dangling from her mouth. When she thought no one was looking, she dipped the toothpick into a snuff box and put it back in her mouth.

Elvis went into her room every night to give her a good night kiss. She never joined us at night in the living room because she went to bed early. I imagine the big groups and singing were too noisy to suit her, but Grandma didn't complain. She understood her place in the house and role in the family.

If Elvis wanted a snack after Grandma went to sleep, I stepped up to bat. Elvis didn't care for chips or peanuts, so I would fix him a peanut butter and banana sandwich. After making more of them than I could count, just the thought of making one today is enough to make me gag. Not that I get many requests for them.

When Elvis was off on maneuvers, I offered to do some cooking to give Grandma a break. Since Elvis had such a limited variety of foods he would eat, I always cooked something different when he was away. Red and Lamar were quite pleased to have a change. Sometimes the three of us would go out to a German *gasthaus* and enjoy some fine German food such as wiener schnitzel with pommes frites (French fries), sauerbraten with potato balls, or bratwurst with sauerkraut. These nights out also allowed me a well-deserved break from my responsibilities at the house.

I received many phone calls and letters from various media publications and radio shows requesting an interview about what it was like being the private secretary for Elvis. I knew that Elvis did not allow anyone from our inner circle to give interviews, or even talk with the press. So I always declined the offers.

A reporter from *Motion Picture Magazine* named Beverly Ott regularly called me from the States. She was quite persistent, and even offered to come over to Germany for a story she wanted to title, "Elvis' Secretary."

I finally told Vernon about her constant phone calls. "Let me talk to Elvis about this," Vernon said, surprising me. I was even more astounded when Elvis gave me the go-ahead for the interview. However, he did have one stipulation: no pictures. He didn't give an explanation or a reason, so the magazine sent a sketch artist in place of a photographer.

Ms. Ott flew to Germany and interviewed me for an entire afternoon at the house in Bad Nauheim. She asked me to describe in detail what it was like being Elvis Presley's personal secretary.

Three months later, she mailed me the magazine that featured the article with my interview. I was disappointed because it was a typical fluff piece. Not only that, but it turned out to be only about 20 percent accurate. She wrote, "Then there's the man who stops by to tune the piano," I was quoted as saying. "At times like these, you might say the job's more like Miltown than Stardust!" The fact is, during the entire time we lived in Bad Nauheim, the piano was never tuned, nor was a piano tuner ever in the house, and I had never used the words Miltown or Stardust.

Ms. Ott also claimed in the article that my five-year-old sister Linda had a crush on Elvis. Although Elvis had shown up at my door previously, my sister had no knowledge of who he was.

Ms. Ott's creative muse: "When they met, Linda looked up at Elvis. He looked down at her. He took her hand. She smiled her shy smile, he smiled his gentle smile. That was it!" Ott wrote, making the exchange sound like something out of a wild romance novel.

This was my first hands-on experience with the press, and it was a major letdown. I showed Elvis the magazine and pointed out the blatant fiction.

"Foghorn, now you know how I feel all the time," Elvis said laughing. He had come to the point where he would say, "Believe nothing you hear or read, and only about half of what you see with your own eyes, and maybe you will be near the truth."

It was a rude awakening to discover some members of the press would write anything just to sell papers and magazines. I could now fully understand why Elvis guarded his privacy and was cautious of whom he trusted.

It was because Elvis hardly trusted anyone that he rarely went anywhere without his bodyguards or Army buddies. So, I was surprised when one afternoon Elvis asked me to escort him out in public.

"Let's just you and me go shopping, Foghorn," Elvis said. I was taken aback, yet overwhelmed with joy. He was looking for a store that had all kinds of knick-knacks.

At the store, Elvis asked me to tell the German saleslady that he was looking for a small trash can for his bedroom. I instantly and unthinkingly blurted out to Elvis that he didn't need one because he already had one in his bedroom, and found out right then that when Elvis Presley wanted an opinion, he'd ask for it.

"Don't you ever tell me what to or what not to buy, and if I want a thousand trash cans in my bedroom, that's my business," he snapped. I was dumbfounded and didn't know how to respond. Elvis grabbed my hand and we abruptly left the store empty-handed.

Our shopping trip had lasted all of five minutes. He was very angry with me. I apologized to him when we got home, even though I wasn't quite sure why I should apologize.

"Foghorn, I had planned on buying you a bunch of new

clothes when we were finished," he pouted. "But now you've ruined it!"

On top of that, he gave me the silent treatment for the next few days. I came to understand from that experience that no matter what, you didn't tell Elvis Presley what to do. This was a side of him I had never seen before, and a side I didn't care to see again. I sure could have used a new wardrobe, but the offer was never made again.

Another shopping trip ended badly for me a week before Easter of 1959. Vernon invited me to go along to Frankfurt to the PX and commissary for groceries and goods. Frankfurt had a much larger PX and commissary than the one in Friedberg, so for major supplies, the Presleys opted to go there.

On our way back to Bad Nauheim, we were traveling north on the Frankfurt-Kassel Autobahn when Vernon attempted to pass another car. Suddenly, a car pulled out in front of us to pass a truck that was in front of both our cars. Vernon swerved the black Mercedes and slammed on the brakes to avoid smashing into that car. The Mercedes swerved and fishtailed, spinning out of control. It rolled over several times and finally came to a sudden stop upside-down on the opposite side of the autobahn after it slammed into a tree.

The Mercedes was a total loss and the inside of the car was a terrible mess. Broken eggs, Coke bottles, glass containers, and punctured flour bags were scattered throughout the inside of our car, on our clothes, and in our hair. My head was cut in several places from the broken glass.

It was when we tried to get out of the car that I realized I could not move. I was terrified my back was broken. Other motorists pulled over to help. Vernon, who was not injured, became very concerned for me. He and some others pulled me out of the car and laid me carefully on the ground. Another helpful stranger left the scene to call an ambulance and to notify the Presley home in Bad Nauheim that there had been an accident.

As soon as people on the scene learned that Elvis' father was driving the wrecked vehicle, things became even more chaotic than had it been just an average car accident. I was taken to the nearest German Krankenhaus (hospital) while Vernon stayed at the scene of the accident. They took me through the emergency entrance and I was put through a series of X-rays. They disclosed that my back and several other areas of my body were badly bruised. Thank God — no broken bones! After I was given clearance from the doctors a few hours later, the ambulance took me back to Goethestrasse 14.

As soon as Elvis, Lamar, and Red heard the news, they raced to the site of the accident. While they were busy tending to Vernon, I arrived home.

Frau Pieper greeted me at the door when I arrived.

"For goodness' sake child! What happened to you?" she asked. My appearance must have horrified her. Before I could answer her, she ordered the drivers to help me into her bedroom. She was also concerned for my health.

When the guys got back, Red and Lamar rushed into her room to check on my condition. It was easy to see that they were genuinely concerned about me. They hugged me and told me what a close call it had been.

I wish Elvis' reaction had been the same. When he came into Frau Pieper's room to see me, he didn't even bother to ask me how I was feeling. Instead, he shook me up almost as badly as the accident with a question out of left field.

"Foghorn, be straight with me," Elvis said right away. "Were you and my daddy messing around with each other while he was driving the car?"

I was absolutely appalled, and deeply hurt by his question, which was really an accusation. I was miserable, still covered in food, and half drugged out of my skull. His question sickened me, but I was in no shape to respond. I was madly in love with Elvis, and Vernon never even entered my mind that way. But Elvis was suspicious of everybody around him, including his own father. Thirty minutes later, a whole different Elvis came in the room.

"Foghorn, are you doing okay?" he asked now with genuine concern. I told him that I was fine, and he said he was glad I wasn't seriously hurt. Elvis told me when he saw the condition of the car, his heart had nearly stopped. He said that he had a sick feeling inside thinking that now he had lost his daddy, too. Foreseeing that the accident would make the local papers, he wanted me to let my parents know I was fine. Elvis and Red hoisted me out of bed so I could use the telephone and call them.

Typically, German newspapers reported that Elvis himself was killed in the car accident. Other headlines read, "Elvis' Father Hurt in Wreck." While all the stories went on about how lucky Vernon was to have escaped death, my name wasn't even mentioned even though I was the one who was the most seriously hurt.

As I lay there in bed, the crash replayed over and over in my head. I couldn't help but think about the car rolling over and smashing into the tree. I visualized being stuck upside-down in the car, staring at all the little cracks in the windshield of the Mercedes.

Then I began to see the irony of the situation — these little cracks symbolized the cracks forming in my relationship with Elvis.

CHAPTER ELEVEN

Cars, Kicks, and Pills

Rex

In my company, I was almost a celebrity myself just because I was a friend to Elvis. The guys at the Kaserne eventually became accustomed to my visits to the Presley house. I never got any teasing from anybody, only envy. Every guy in my outfit would have killed to trade places with me. They thought Elvis and I had been friends before our military service because we were drafted the same day and were both from the same general area. Little did they know we actually met on the day we were inducted. The guys were always asking me to get autographs or pictures of Elvis for them. Everyone wanted a piece of him.

Like everyone else in Germany, the Bavarian Motor Works of Munich also wanted a little piece of Elvis. When I had visited Graceland, Elvis proudly showed me his collection of cars, which included many expensive Cadillacs.

I discovered Elvis had quite a history with cars.

"If we were to get around at all, it was up to me to do my own driving," Elvis said. He confessed to me that during World War II while Vernon was off working in Memphis, he started driving his mother around when he was only 10 years old.

One time, Elvis gave his mother a good scare when he parked at a store and he mistook the "drive" for "reverse" on the gear shift and released the clutch. The car shot up onto the curb and nearly went through the store window, but Elvis' cool managed to stop just in the nick of time.

Elvis' next experience behind the wheel occurred after the Presley family moved to Memphis, and traveled back to Tupelo for an occasional visit. They owned an older Pontiac whose accelerator was so stiff that when Vernon's foot got tired, Elvis would sit in the middle of the car seat and feed the gas while Vernon steered.

By the age of 17, Elvis obtained his driver's license by borrowing his Uncle Travis Smith's car to take the test. He passed with flying colors.

"After that, there was no keeping him away from the wheel," Vernon recalled.

Elvis purchased his first car after he performed a string of sellout shows in the South. Elvis liked both his cars and his clothes flashy. He purchased a used 1954 four-door pink and white Cadillac.

According to Elvis, that Caddy met an untimely demise when its handbrake caused it to catch fire after a gig in Hope, Arkansas, in June, 1954. Elvis was riding with a date when several cars and truck drivers passed him and honked their horns to let him know something was wrong.

"By the time I pulled over, the entire rear of the car was ablaze," Elvis said.

A bus full of passengers pulled over to the side of the road and tried to help, but it was too late. The car was engulfed in flames. Elvis fought the good fight until someone pulled him away seconds before the gas tank exploded.

Elvis was heartbroken and terribly distraught when he returned to Memphis without his beloved Caddy. He sulked for days.

"Man, I loved that car," Elvis said with a far-off look in his eye.

As Elvis' popularity grew, so did his Cadillac collection. Elvis soon bought another car, the famous 1955 pink and black Cadillac he bought for his mother, Gladys. This Cadillac was in all the entertainment magazines early on in his career. By the time I knew Elvis, the Cadillac count was up to four.

I believe cars were the first things he bought when he started making money. In subsequent years he also collected guns, badges, jewelry, and flashy clothes to satisfy his need for toys. Other things, too.

"You might say cars and women are my two favorite hobbies," Elvis said with a wink. "Probably in that order."

When Elvis set his eyes on a sporty white limited edition BMW 507 with rich leather interior, Gloeckle's BMW showroom saw a tremendous promotional opportunity.

The vehicle, originally driven by a famous German roadster, was selling for $7,160. Knowing Elvis would be an ideal poster boy, they offered Elvis the special low price of $3,750. Famous German game show hostess Uschi Siebert was contracted to give Elvis his new car keys in front of the media. The dealership made it into a big event, which was captured in many photos and made big headlines in the newspapers.

It was not Elvis, but rather Vernon, who actually drove the BMW back to Bad Nauheim. Elvis followed closely behind in his Mercedes with Lamar and Red as passengers. On their way back photographers were hot on the trail, so Vernon attempted to lose them by speeding through railroad gates just in the nick of time. The Mercedes wasn't so lucky, and wound up wedged between the gates, on train tracks. With the train heading their way, somehow Elvis steered the car out of harm's way.

But the Mercedes was living on borrowed time. Shortly after this episode it was destroyed while Vernon was driving it on the autobahn. The fate of the BMW was slightly less gruesome.

When Elvis had signed the agreement for the BMW, he couldn't read it since it was written in German. He assumed it was his car to keep, but the $3,750 he paid to Gloceckle was actually for a lease. The dealership wanted the car back when he left Germany.

To make matters worse, some fans ruined the paint job on the BMW by writing messages to Elvis on the car. Elvis had to have it painted red to camouflage the graffiti. When the car was finally returned to the dealership, the company painted it back to the original white color. Since they were less than thrilled about the situation, they unsuccessfully tried to bill Elvis for the final paint job.

Fast moves intrigued Elvis even when he wasn't behind the wheel. Around this time, he began taking an interest in the martial art called karate. In early December, 1958, Elvis and I attended a karate demonstration given by Jurgen Seydel, known as "The Father of German Karate." We were both very impressed as we watched Seydel demonstrate his fighting maneuvers.

After the demonstration, Elvis immediately signed us up and we began taking formal karate lessons at Swaddles Studio in Bad Homburg. I was excited to learn a new craft and honored that Elvis included me. It was not often that someone had time alone with Elvis, so this was a good opportunity for our friendship to blossom. Elvis mentioned he had always been interested in karate, but never had the time or financial means to do anything about it.

At first, Elvis and I went twice a week. Before long, Elvis was giving demonstrations and lectures on the discipline required to master the art of karate and on its superiority over other forms of martial arts. Since I was fast on my feet and well-coordinated physically, Elvis picked me to be his sparring partner in class.

Seydel was always cool and professional. He didn't get caught up in the fact that one of his students was an international celebrity. I think Elvis admired Seydel's confidence and ability. The major emphasis of Seydel's classes was self-defense. He was opposed to getting into fights. Seydel preached doing everything possible to avoid an altercation, but said if there was no choice it was best to know how to defend yourself. Elvis proved an apt student.

"He had an incredible capacity for perception and was one of my most talented pupils," Seydel said about Elvis.

Elvis was committed to learning karate and practiced whenever he could. He also took additional classes when he knew I wasn't around so he could get ahead of me. Sometimes Seydel came to the house on Goethestrasse 14 and gave Elvis private karate lessons. The furniture was moved out of the way and the living room became the karate studio. In addition to acting as Elvis' practice partner, I became his dummy when he wanted to show off his new karate moves. He did all the narration, explaining the moves as we demonstrated them. Elvis was always the aggressor and I was the defender. This gave me the chance to show off my defensive skills. Our audience could feel Elvis' excitement and always cheered him on.

He was fascinated by the dangerous elements of karate. For instance, a skillful martial artist could smash his enemy's face with the palm of his hand and drive the bone from his nose into his brain, instantly killing him. A person could also be blinded by a deliberate karate chop. Elvis had a thing about wanting to show everybody how tough he could be.

Elvis didn't use karate to split wood, but he sure loved to practice the art of looking dangerous. Elvis was double-jointed and this gave him a menacing appearance in the dojo. In later years he incorporated karate moves into his concerts.

There was also a more practical side to his karate study. He expressed a constant fear that some jealous boyfriend would approach him in anger, as had been done in the past. Elvis told me that even before the Army, some had come after him with knives and guns. Countless times, Red was forced to restrain somebody who wanted to take a poke at Elvis, which is one of the reasons Elvis liked having Red in his corner. Elvis admired Red's bravery and fearless attitude in potentially dangerous situations, but he didn't want to count on him all the time.

Red never thought twice about protecting or defending Elvis. One example of this occurred after Elvis had words with a Military Police officer. Elvis was driving the BMW off-base when he was stopped by the nasty MP, who started harassing Elvis for, of all things, having mud on his license plate. Obviously, this guy was really enjoying pushing Elvis around. He was probably jealous of Elvis and his car, and was using his authority to rub Elvis' nose in it.

When Elvis arrived home in a foul mood, he explained what had happened.

"That sonofabitch of an MP tried to embarrass me for no reason. I'd like to kick his ass!" he yelled.

That was all Red needed to hear, and then he wanted to kick the guy's ass, too. After Elvis described what the MP looked like,

Red figured out who he was. The MP happened to be a regular at Beck's Bar, Red's favorite hangout.

In no time, Red was on his way there. The MP was on the premises, and he did not look happy when he saw Red coming toward him. Red's reputation obviously preceded him. The guy admitted he had pushed his luck with Elvis and tried making amends with Red. Red insisted he come back to the Presley house to work things out with Elvis directly. There was no talking him out of it.

"Is this the guy who was giving you all that shit?" Red asked Elvis after they arrived. Then Red left the living room, leaving the two men alone. After a few minutes, the MP emerged from the house with a towel in his hand. He went to the BMW, stooped down and wiped the offending mud off the license plate as Elvis, watching from the window, sported a wide smile.

Unfortunately, the high Elvis got from his karate exertions wasn't enough. When I first started coming to the house on Goethestrasse 14, I was introduced to this magical little white pill. It was an amphetamine called Dexedrine. This was the first time I became aware that Elvis was taking any pills. I don't know how long he had been taking them, but he appeared to be very knowledgeable on the subject. His mother had been taking these pills for "diet control." Maybe this was how he was first introduced to this drug, but I was not at all familiar with amphetamines.

It was also known that while we were in Grafenwohr, a sergeant gave Elvis and some other GI's pills to keep them energized. On certain maneuvers, the GI's were required to stay up through the night, and the sergeant didn't want anybody falling asleep on the job. Elvis liked how these pills made him feel. Whatever Elvis' history with amphetamines was, he was well-versed concerning their effects. Elvis acted like a doctor when prescribing them for me, and I believed everything Elvis said about these white pills.

"Rex, truck drivers back in the States use these all the time to stay awake on long trips," Elvis informed me. "Plus, they have no side effects." Elvis told me Red and Lamar were also taking these pills, which made his testimonial more convincing to me. I figured why not?

"Rexadus, it's a whole lot better to take the pill with coffee. The hot coffee and caffeine will make the pill kick in quicker," Elvis said. He demonstrated for me by swallowing a pill and gulping down his caffeine chaser. Elvis assured me the pills were completely harmless.

"Don't worry, Rexadus, once you eat something, the effect wears right off," Elvis said handing me my first dose.

I had no reason to doubt a word Elvis said, and gladly accepted my bottle of amphetamines from his supply. Besides, Doc Presley also informed me that these pills would keep a person trim because they were appetite suppressants prescribed by doctors to millions of overweight people every day.

After taking my first pill, I actually felt the hair on my head standing up and a surge of energy bolting through my body. Elvis was completely right about one thing — that white pill provided me with an abundance of strength and energy I didn't know I had. I could take them and stay awake an entire weekend. I was astonished that after taking only one pill, I could easily go 24 hours without food or sleep. And they were harmless!

The problem with any drug is that a person's body eventually gets used to it, and must have even larger quantities to feel the same effect. In just a few weeks, I had worked my way up to two pills a day. And that was just Monday through Friday. Weekends required additional assistance. The routine started with the usual two pills Friday morning; then we added two pills on Friday night. The same dosage was taken on Saturday. Two pills were again taken on Sunday morning; then we would wind down for the new week. On Monday, when it came time to soldier again, I felt wrung out. So we had to take a few more pills, and the energy would return. It became a vicious cycle. Eventually I dropped down to 140 pounds, which was my high school weight.

Vernon was aware of our involvement with amphetamines and on rare occasions took them himself. Even Elisabeth knew about the pills, but Elvis must also have convinced her they were harmless. On the nights that we went to clubs in Frankfurt, Elvis would give Elisabeth a few pills. Those were the only instances she ever used them. I am not sure whether Grandma knew what was going on. I can only imagine what she would've been like on the little buggers.

Elvis must have kept a tremendous stash of amphetamines because anytime I ran out he always had another hundred or so to give me. None of us knew where he stored his supply. I never noticed any in the bathroom, and I figured he hid them in his bedroom.

I always wondered where on earth he was getting this endless supply. Then one Friday afternoon I was riding home with Elvis for the weekend. We stopped by the post dispensary, which is the military pharmacy on post. I don't know how much Elvis was paying the guy at the dispensary, but I saw some large bills change hands. This guy handed Elvis about four quart-sized bottles filled up with Dexedrine.

"Rexadus, it ain't what you know but who you know that counts in this old world," Elvis said with a wink. He should have added, "And if you got lots of money, it helps."

Dexedrine is a controlled substance with a high potential for addiction. But back then it was common for people to take this drug to reduce and maintain weight. It was also recommended for people who were seriously depressed. These "uppers" cause a temporary mood elevation. This effect will occur even in people who are not depressed. After the stimulant wears off, there is a let-down, or "crash" period. People who abuse stimulants also build up a tolerance, and the dose must be increased to achieve the same effect. It doesn't take long for someone to become dependent on amphetamines. At the time we were taking the pills, there was not a lot of information available on them. It's only been in the past few decades that research showed how dangerous these pills are.

I'll have to say that Elvis never forced me to take the pills; nor did I take the time to research them. I do not blame Elvis in any way for turning me on to uppers. After the Army, I continued to take amphetamines with a doctor's prescription. I was addicted, and it took five long years for me to kick the habit.

As we know, Elvis was unable to control his addiction to prescription drugs, and it ultimately lead to his demise. I understand he took a wide variety of pills up to the day of his death.

My dependency on drugs took a toll on me physically and emotionally, and affected my personal relationships. I can only imagine what it did to Elvis after so many years.

Back in Germany, of course, we were hardly worried about what the drugs were doing to our bodies. We were popping pills, having the time of our lives, and feeling no pain.

CHAPTER TWELVE

Domestic Bliss

Rex

When the clan moved to Goethestrasse 14, I began visiting on a regular basis. Elvis told me to come and stay overnight anytime I could get a pass, and on the weekends I became a full-time resident.

"Rexadus, my home will be your home away from home," Elvis said with all sincerity. He made me feel that I was an important part of his family. He made Charlie Hodge feel just as welcome. Elvis, Vernon, Grandma, Red, Lamar, Charlie, Elisabeth, and I were now a tight-knit group. There were others who shuffled in and out, but we comprised the basis of Elvis' inner circle during his stint in Germany.

We had plenty of fun in that house at Goethestrasse 14, singing and harmonizing together. Elvis would play the piano while Charlie played the guitar. Red could pick and sing pretty well, and the rest of us could carry a tune. Even Vernon would join in occasionally with his Grand Ole Opry style voice, which sounded pretty good. I had a high tenor voice and Elvis always tried to get me to hit my highest note. Actually, we weren't all that bad as a group, and we had a lot of good old-fashioned fun.

When we weren't singing, Elvis moved the fun outdoors. He and Red were both crazy about football. From what they told me, Red was an all-state football player in high school. Elvis and Red were continually organizing football games with other GI's on Sunday afternoons. We played in a big field, not far from the house, which was next to an old water purifying system. This was the purified water that was used for the health baths that so many people came to the area to enjoy.

I was a well-coordinated athlete myself and had played a lot of basketball and baseball during my high school years. In Germany we were playing American football, not German football — which was soccer. Our games were supposed to be "touch football," but actually they were much rougher. Elvis had a habit of picking the biggest and toughest guys from the Kaserne for the opposing team, so that he could show how tough he was. The strange part was that nobody got injured, which is amazing considering our hell-bent-for-leather style of play.

I played wide receiver because I was very fast on my feet. It was during one of our football games that Red finally accepted me as an equal. I ran out for a pass from Elvis, and Red made a great block, which gave me a chance to run full speed downfield. Elvis threw a perfect pass just barely over the head of the defender covering me. I caught the ball over my shoulder while running full stride. At about the same time, I ran into a split-rail fence about 18 inches high. The fence happened to be the end of our football field, and we would have to jump over it to score. It presented a few problems, but only a minor inconvenience in this instance.

Since I was looking over my shoulder to catch that pass thrown by Elvis, I didn't see what was in front of me. Both shins slammed into the fence with a loud cracking sound and I did a somersault in mid-air. To everyone's amazement including my own, I somehow hung onto the football, and it turned out to be the winning touchdown for our team. Both Elvis and Red couldn't get over that I hadn't dropped the ball. Red seemed particularly impressed, and after that evinced a new respect for me. For a couple of weeks, Elvis and Red would verbally replay that touchdown to all the guests at the house. They made me out as their hero, which of course made me feel pretty darn good about myself.

While Elvis and I were equals on the football field, back at the post I actually held a higher rank. We were each promoted to our next higher rank every time we had enough time in grade, which referred to the length of time one had to stay at a particular rank before being promoted. Because of my prior military service in the Tennessee National Guard, my official promotions would always come a couple of months before Elvis'. However, Elvis was a jeep driver in the Scouts Headquarters Company, and I was a tank commander in C Company of our 32nd Armored Battalion — his duties as a jeep driver and scout were fairly simple as long as we were not in actual combat. In combat situations, Elvis would have been more exposed to greater possible injury or death as the scouts were positioned in front of the tanks to keep an eye out for a surprise attack.

My duties were more complicated and intense on a daily basis, as I had responsibility for the tank and the crew. Elvis had to sign a government document that he would be responsible for the jeep and its equipment, which included a 50-caliber machine gun. I also had to sign a document, but it was for a tank and its equipment and ammunition. The jeep and equipment were probably valued at $10,000 (in 1959 dollars). The M-50 tank, complete with the machine guns, ammo, and communications equipment, probably had a value of around $300,000.

The documents we personally signed held us responsible for the government's property if anything was destroyed or lost due to negligence. Before Uncle Sam let us leave the Army, all the equipment we signed out had to be accounted for. Needless to say, it was a huge responsibility and made me very nervous to have to sign this document.

I was in charge of a four-man crew and responsible for keeping myself and the tank ready for combat at all times. Usually the tanks had a four-man crew, which made the workload easier. On the headquarters' tank, there were only three men required since the company commander had to take over the leadership post during field maneuvers and alerts. During these training exercises and mock combat situations, I would become the gunner on the tank. That meant that I had to be proficient as a both a tank commander and a gunner, and was tested accordingly.

We had an inspection every month, and every piece of ammo had to be laid out on the ground on the tarp. The ammo consisted of 50 rounds of 90-mm gun shells, 500 rounds of 50-caliber, and 1,000 rounds of 30-caliber ammo. Also, the machine guns had to be dismounted and laid out alongside the ammo for inspection. Not so much as a speck of dust was allowed to be on any of the weapons or ammo. Everything on that tank had to be shined and polished.

Our company commander, Lieutenant Patton, who was promoted to Captain early during our tenure at Ray Barracks in Friedberg, did not believe in second place. Our C Company usually placed first in the inspections. If we lost, there was hell to pay — an entire month of trial inspections until we got it absolutely perfect. The next inspection was our chance to redeem ourselves for a past disgrace.

The record will show that C Company was the best overall performing company in the 32nd Armor Battalion. Also, it was common practice in the tank corps for the best tank crew to be on the company commander's tank. Bragging ain't bragging if you can prove it.

Clearly then, my responsibilities and duties were weightier than Elvis' during our tour of duty in Germany. On the other hand, I didn't postpone my civilian job as the world's greatest entertainer.

Elvis never said anything about my becoming a tank commander and wearing sergeant stripes before him, but I certainly could detect a little resentment coming from his direction. "Now Rexadus, don't be gettin' all gung-ho on me now that you're a hotshot sergeant," he kidded me on the square. The term "gung-ho" was a military expression for a soldier who followed his orders with precision and did his job with perfection and pride. "Horse's ass" could be another way to put it.

My sergeant stripes also permitted me membership in the NCO club with all the other sergeants. One time I nearly got into a fight because of this privilege. The NCO's accepted me without question because they saw my stripes, but my identification card showed that I was below the rank of sergeant. This meant that I could also go to the enlisted men's club as long as I wore civvies. The latter club was located on a hill above our living quarters. It was a large building which resembled an airplane hangar and could hold up to a thousand soldiers on any given night.

One of my crew members was having a birthday party and wanted me to join the crew at the enlisted men's club for a beer. I put on my civilian clothes and joined them. There were about seven of us sitting at a table when a guy next to us began shooting off his mouth. He was a drunk who had been busted down from sergeant to private because of problems directly connected to his fondness for booze. Before that happened, he had spotted me at the NCO club; now my presence at the enlisted men's club fired up his resentment.

"Hey, what's that gung-ho sergeant bastard doing in here?" he yelled so that everyone in the place could hear him. Then he got up and headed toward me, acting as if he were going to do me physical harm. Every member of my tank crew stood up while I remained seated.

"If you come one step closer, we're going to tear your head off," one of my guys told him. The soldiers who were with this drunk came over quickly and dragged him back to their table. He was still carrying on when the Military Police ushered him out. He spent the night in the brig for trying to start a fight. A ban on fighting among the soldiers was strictly enforced and punishable by the military code of justice. If anyone had a grievance with another soldier, and it could not be resolved peacefully, they were given a pair of boxing gloves and told to settle it in the ring at the base gym.

The reason I was a tank commander and wore sergeant stripes before officially becoming one was that I was what the Army calls an "acting sergeant." There were always a few acting sergeants in every outfit. They were soldiers who were good leaders and knew how to handle the job, but did not have enough time in grade to be officially promoted. In other words, I did the job of a sergeant, but received the pay of a corporal. This may not sound fair, but the rank held a few fringe benefits, such as not pulling guard duty, extra time off, and NCO club privileges. When you have been around long enough, you learn the ropes.

One of the tricks that Elvis and I played on new recruits, which had been done to us when we first arrived, was to send them on an errand to find a hydrostatic-lock key. All tank-type vehicles with the big V-12 Chrysler engines at that time had the possibility of locking up. It was caused by excess gasoline gathering on top of the engine cylinders. If this occurred when the engine was first being turned by the starter, which engaged the magneto firing apparatus too quickly, the gasoline could explode, causing the engine to lock up. This was called a hydrostatic lock, and the engine would have to be taken apart and rebuilt before it would run again. If you didn't start the V-12 Chrysler engines exactly according to procedure, the tanks were prone to this problem.

Obviously, there is no such thing as a "hydrostatic-lock" key. Except for the new recruits, every soldier from the Colonel on down knew and would gladly participate in this joke. We would send the poor recruit all over the Kaserne looking for these keys. After a few days, the recruits would eventually learn that they were being played for a sucker, and once they figured that out they could not wait for the next new recruit to come along so they could give him a taste of the same medicine. Some of these poor guys would go nearly nuts trying to find that "key."

Another story Elvis always got a kick out of was the one about the snow snakes of Germany. Again, this was always told to the new recruits, and it was surprising how many would swallow it right up to the punchline.

We started by telling the new guys when we had to go to the field for maneuvers and there was snow on the ground, so be sure to watch out for deadly snow snakes. These deadly reptiles, we'd warn, would crawl from their snow-covered burrows into your sleeping bag at night. Before you could stop them, a snake would crawl up your tailhole and freeze you to death. As soon as the punchline was reached, usually they'd figure out the whole thing was a joke. Typically this joke would be told to one new recruit at a time, while several of the older seasoned GI's were gathered around. This would give everybody a hearty laugh at the new recruit's expense.

Elvis fit in well and performed his duties, whether at Ray Barracks or on maneuvers. He was just like all the other soldiers, and he was conscientious about being on time, and never left early. The only difference was that he lived off-base. Elvis went home everyday for lunch, mainly because he hated to stand in the chow lines. Actually, he never had any peace in the line because everybody was always watching him and wanting to talk with him. I don't blame him for going home to Bad Nauheim for lunch.

As a matter of fact, the only line Elvis got into was the one that formed when GI's lined up once a month to be paid. Other GI's would come by him in line to pay back money they'd borrowed. Elvis was a real pushover when it came to loaning money to the GI's in his outfit, and couldn't turn them down. The amount of the loans averaged about $20 each, usually made right before payday, which came only once a month. On payday, Elvis would get back the $200 to $300 he had loaned out. Most of the time, he did not even know everybody to whom he had loaned money. I know some of those guys took advantage of Elvis and never paid him back, but he never complained. He used to say he understood their needs and was glad to help out.

Not only was he extremely generous, he was also extremely busy with the ladies.

Elvis met an actress, 18-year-old Vera Tschechowa, at a charity event back in January of 1959. She came to visit him at

Goethestrasse 14 and invited all of us to the local movie house to see one of her films. Elvis was curious to see just what kind of actress she was.

Oddly enough, Janie Wilbanks was with us when we went to the movies. Elisabeth also came along as Elvis' translator, and she gave Elvis a running account of what the movie was about.

Vera's mother and grandmother were also actresses. I think seeing Elvis was nothing more to her than a simple publicity stunt. The papers made it appear as if there were some big, passionate romance taking place. The fact is, Elvis would shy away from celebrity types, because they were usually only after publicity for themselves.

In early March, Elvis, Lamar, and Red traveled to Munich for a brief visit with Vera, and attended a theatrical performance she was in. The three of them sat through the whole play which was entirely in German. They later frequented a burlesque club called Moulin Rouge, which they undoubtedly enjoyed much more.

We also had our favorite places closer to Bad Nauheim. Occasionally on Friday or Saturday nights the whole group went to various nightclubs in Frankfurt, which was about 30 miles away. Beer and liquor were banned from the house because Elvis did not drink alcohol at this time. According to him, nobody else should drink, either. I think he had been affected by his family's alcoholism in some way and it brought back sad memories for him. Prescription drugs, obviously, were a whole different matter.

The only beverages I remember seeing Elvis drink were coffee, soda, and water. On our nights out with him, we would sneak a drink while the show was in progress and the lights down low. Elvis wouldn't notice because he usually had a table full of girls. I figured Elvis knew we were having a drink, but didn't say anything. In fact, when Vernon joined us on these nightclub trips, he would sneak a drink with the rest of us boys. He was quite fond of his toddies.

Once in a while, Elisabeth would also join us for a weekend night at a club, which was a bad idea because Elvis would usually end up bringing another girl home with him. This was terribly deflating for Elisabeth. She would roll her eyes at the rest of us when Elvis wasn't looking. Sometimes she looked like she was about to cry. We all felt sorry for her and wished Elvis would not subject Elisabeth to such nonchalant cruelty.

In the middle of March, a knee injury knocked Elvis out of commission for three days. He was thrown from a jeep that took a rough turn. Elvis preferred that the press not be notified, so it remained fairly confidential.

He recovered nicely by March 27, in time to host an "Over the Hump" party on the base for his headquarters' company platoon, to commemorate the halfway point of our hitch in Germany.

This got me thinking about how much we had been through together. It had been a heady, exciting ride, that's for sure. I didn't know what Part Two would bring, but this traveling salesman was in for the duration. Or, at least until the King of Rock and Roll decided otherwise.

CHAPTER THIRTEEN

Parlez-Vous Français?

Rex

In May 1959, Red West went back to Memphis. Red told me later that he was tired of Elvis treating him like a "Chinese coolie," and paying him no better than an indentured slave. Red had too much pride to ask Elvis for money, and Elvis wasn't too concerned about Red's financial situation. It got so bad sometimes that Red couldn't even buy a beer.

Accordingly, Red went back to the United States and did not return again while Elvis was in Germany. After Red went back to Memphis, a guy named Cliff Gleaves stepped in to replace him.

Army life was rigorous, and I was always ready to escape from the daily grind. It was perfect timing when Elvis asked me if I could take some leave and go with him to Munich and Paris. I jumped at the chance and requested a 14-day leave. Elvis had picked the dates and invited Lamar and Charlie to come along with us. I learned that we would be going by train, first-class, to Paris via Munich.

On June 13, 1959, the four of us boarded the train. We had one common goal for this trip — fun! Fortunately for us, Elvis paid for

137

everything. Even combining our money, the rest of us would never have been able to afford this kind of vacation. Our private compartment was very fancy, and we had plenty of space. "This is the life. Now boys, we are gonna live it up," Elvis said, leaning back, kicking his feet up and lighting a cigar.

The train ride lasted about four hours. We ate from the snack cart and smoked cigars the entire trip. When we detrained there, a limousine was waiting to take us to our hotel. Lamar had made arrangements before we left, and the driver was at our complete disposal the entire time we were in Munich.

Our first night there was by far the most memorable. We went to the famous Moulin Rouge Night Club. We were escorted to the balcony after the first show and were shown to separate booths. As usual, Elvis had two or three beauties in his booth, while the rest of us were satisfied to have just one. Incidentally, the girls were part of the show. We had picked them out while viewing their acts. While we dallied with them, a new set of girls were showing off their well-maintained figures on stage. We could see what was going on downstairs from the balcony.

"Now that I already got mine, pick out any girl you like," Elvis had said with a smile, generously sharing his wealth.

I picked out a cutie who reminded me of Brigitte Bardot. I was just sitting there with her, sipping champagne, minding my own business, and soaking in the moment, when I noticed a guy was standing at the entrance to my booth. He must have been over six feet tall. He started very calmly speaking in German to my new friend. I got the feeling he was her boyfriend and wanted her to leave with him, but it was apparent she didn't want to.

"Do you need any help?" I asked her. She didn't respond to that, but stayed beside me shaking her head at the guy in the doorway. Next thing I knew, he was inside pulling this defense-less girl up by her arms and out of the booth. What really angered me was that he then shoved her down on the floor and began pushing her down the archway.

"That ain't no way to treat a lady," I said, getting up myself.

I caught up with them at the door of the balcony, which led out first to a foyer and then to the stairs. I grabbed the boyfriend's shoulder, and as he turned toward me, his fist slammed into my jaw extremely hard. Guessing he wasn't in the mood to talk things over, I punched back and the two of us stood there toe-to-toe, trading blows.

Things were getting completely out of control when a cooler head intervened. It was, in fact, the coolest head in rock and roll.

"OK MEN, NOW LET'S BREAK IT UP," said Elvis in a loud booming voice. Then, as Hans or whatever his name was dropped his fists, Elvis turned to me and whispered, "Rexadus, now hit him good!"

I missed my cue, so Elvis tried again. "Break it up, now, break it up," he ordered, and then again turned to me and quietly said, "Kill him, Rex! Kill the bastard!"

To make things easier for me, Elvis grabbed my dumbfounded (and plain dumb) opponent's arms and pinned him against the wall. I didn't need to be told a third time. My eyes narrowed and I took in a deep breath then I drew my fist back like a baseball pitcher's wind up and let it fly. It landed on his jaw and the sap went out like a light as Elvis turned him loose to slide down the wall. Lamar and Charlie showed up just in time to witness my grand slam.

Although it seemed like a 15-rounder to me, the fight was actu-ally over before the manager of the club even arrived on the scene. By the time he got to us, Elvis was ready for him.

"I sure do apologize for this situation, sir, but this guy got a little out of hand and my boys had to put him in his place," Elvis said in a calming and apologetic manner. Too bad the Paramount folks weren't there to witness his performance. It was so Oscar-worthy that the manager apologized to us for any inconvenience.

Some club employees hauled my victim away, and the girl from my booth followed them out. We were told she was later seen driving the car away, because her boyfriend was still out cold. Neither was welcomed back; the girl was fired.

As for us, we decided to prepare ourselves in case Hans rounded up some pals to wait for us outside the club. When we left, each of us carried out a large ashtray that would've done serious damage bouncing off even a thick Teutonic skull. But the coast was clear, and we motioned for the girls to join us in the car. Fortunately, the incident never made the papers.

Normally, I am not a fighter. That's not to say I would run away from a fight, but I would avoid one if at all possible. But there was something about being around Elvis that gave a person a certain recklessness. Maybe it was because Red West was no longer with us, and I wanted Elvis to think I could pick up the slack if called upon. I did it to please him just as much as to defend that girl.

Elvis must have retold that story a hundred times later on. He was showing off, which he was entitled to do, but it also made me look good in front of all the others. Elvis had me completely act out the whole scene over and over for any new people we met. One of the other guys would act as the dummy, and Elvis would hold down his arms and back him against a wall. I then would take my windup and deliver the haymaker — pulled, of course. I'll confess that it tickled me every single time Elvis told the story. It really made me feel like a hero.

After we slept for a few hours, Lamar and I were ready to see a bit of Munich. Elvis and Charlie were not interested, so we had the driver take us to the world-famous Munich Hofbrau Haus, a huge beer hall. This place had long tables and everyone sang along to polkas and Oompah music. The beer was served in one-liter glass steins.

That night, Elvis wanted to go back to the Moulin Rouge. He enjoyed the fight so much he was ready for more action. Although there were no fights the second evening, we still had a lot of fun. We ended up at the hotel with our usual collection of girls before we left in the morning for Paris.

As our driver was heading for the train station, we suddenly realized that Elvis' military dress blue uniform was still at the hotel. By the time we turned around to retrieve it, the train to Paris had left without us.

"Don't worry about it guys, we can catch the train from the next stop down the road," Elvis said with the assurance of someone used to getting his way, which he proposed to do by now offering our driver a deal.

"I'll give ya a hundred bucks if you can outrun the train to the next stop," Elvis told him. Sure enough, we beat the train to the next city. It was an overnight trip to Paris and the private cabins turned into sleepers. We all gathered around Elvis' bed before calling it a night.

"Damn your ass, Lamar, it was your job to make sure we didn't forget that uniform," Elvis said. I felt sorry for poor Lamar and apologized for the incident, too, hoping this would take some of the heat off him. Of course, I avoided pointing out that nobody else had forgotten their dress uniforms. I didn't fancy sleeping on the railroad tracks that night.

When we arrived at the main train station in Paris by mid-morning, we still had 10 full days left of our leave. We were greeted by a man named Jean Aberbach of Hill and Range music publishers. Aberbach was a Viennese refugee with a long history in European music publishing. He had set up Hill and Range in 1945 to celebrate American native folk music. With him was a man named Ben Star, an attorney for the firm.

Both of our hosts were responsible for promoting Elvis on the European market. Colonel Parker had instructed them to take care of his boy in Paris, and do whatever Elvis wanted. Aberbach suggested a guided tour of Paris. Lamar and I wanted to see the tourist sights, but Elvis had no real interest.

"I want to see everything but the normal tourist attractions," Elvis told Aberbach. He was only interested in the nightlife, and that's what we saw the whole time we were in Paris.

We were delivered directly to the plush Hôtel Prince de Galles, which was just about one block away from the famous Champs Élysées, and about three blocks away from the Arc de Triomphe. The Arc de Triomphe was built as a war memorial to the soldiers who gave their lives during the Napoleonic Wars. It was a gigantic structure with a big arch in the center facing down the Champs Élysées. In the center of the Arc, at ground level, was an eternal burning flame.

The traffic laws in Paris permitted vehicles to access the circle around the Arc, but to get off the circle required an act of pure courage. It was dangerous to weave through the maze of cars and peel off on one of the main streets. We were all thankful to have a skilled driver.

Most importantly, we were about two blocks from the famous Lido's Night Club. Our hosts had already booked us into a suite of rooms at the hotel which consisted of two large bedrooms with a parlor. Elvis took one of the bedrooms for himself, Lamar chose the parlor and Charlie and I took the other bedroom. We were on the top floor of the Prince de Galles with a beautiful view of Paris from the windows of our large suite. Aberbach stayed in a room a few floors down from us to keep a watchful eye out. After a couple hours rest and a late lunch, the excitement began.

First on the agenda was a live press conference with the Paris press. Although Elvis had given several press conferences since he had been drafted, I had never attended one. It was different than I expected, more sedate.

The press conference was quite grand and official, and I imagined it would be similar for the President of the United States. It was held in the hotel's finest conference room, and there must have been at least a hundred reporters attending. The television and movie cameras were humming like mad and the flashes from still cameras were blinding. Elvis was seated behind a long table covered with microphones. Lamar, Charlie, and I stood right behind Elvis, as if we had something stately to contribute.

It lasted over an hour. The reporters peppered Elvis with all types of questions.

"Elvis, how do you like Paris?"

"What about Germany?"

"Which are prettier, the girls in France or Germany?"

"Where else will you visit in Europe?"

He did an extraordinary job of interacting with the press and was the consummate professional. I pinched myself to be sure this was really happening. Elvis was so much like one of the guys when he was offstage, but in the spotlight he was transformed. I would have been scared to death if I had been in his shoes. But

Elvis was right at home behind the mass of microphones, and he had a genuine love affair with the French press.

One thing that stands out in my memory of it was the reporters unanimously agreeing that Paris was the most international city in the world. They told Elvis that celebrities could be seen walking down the streets without being bothered or even noticed, much less mobbed by fans. Elvis remarked that he was glad to hear this because, finally, he was in a place where he could be accepted just like any other human being. He even mentioned that he was looking forward to seeing the sights of Paris (although we knew better), including the Eiffel Tower, the Arc of Triumph, the Louvre, Napolean's Tomb, and more. Elvis actually seemed excited by the idea that in Paris, he would be just another face in the crowd. But before he bought the notion wholesale, he wanted to take it for a little test drive.

"Before we make all these plans to tour Paris, let's try her out and see for sure if those reporters were right," Elvis said. We walked out the front door of the hotel in broad daylight and headed for the Champs Élysées. It was a bright, sunny day and the streets were fairly crowded. Sure enough, we walked along peacefully for three whole blocks. There were lots of people who stopped and stared, but nobody rushed for autographs.

"Wow! This is fantastic. We are going to have so much fun here," Elvis commented. But like the snow snakes of Germany, the idea that Elvis Presley could go unnoticed and unbothered anywhere was a giant crock. We came upon this quaint sidewalk café on the Champs Élysées and decided to sit down for refreshments and a little people-watching. Coincidentally, it was called The American Café. All of a sudden, we were mobbed. Out of nowhere, hundreds of people began swarming around us trying to get to Elvis. They all wanted autographs, to take pictures, to touch, or talk with him.

"We got big trouble!" Lamar yelled, going into full body-guard mode.

"Rex, don't touch Elvis, let him get behind you," he yelled, "and he will grab hold. I will get in front of you, Rex, and Charlie, you come up behind Elvis." We followed orders like the obedient GI's we were as Lamar gave the instructions. He was experienced in this type of situation. Jean Aberbach wasn't. He turned pale with fear and started ranting and raving in French.

"Jean, get in the line and let's go!" Lamar ordered. We managed to make a U-turn and ran like hell back to the hotel.

"Yeah, I can really walk down the streets in Paris without anyone bothering me," Elvis said sarcastically as we stood at the elevator to go to our rooms. He rolled his eyes and we all started laughing.

I had never been in the middle of a mob like that before, and it was frightening. This was a classic example of why Elvis needed bodyguards. He would have been in a tough spot if we had not been there to help. Maybe Jerry Lewis could run free in Paris, but Elvis was a different story. He was disappointed that the reporters were wrong, but also secretly thrilled to know he was so popular even in a sophisticated place like Paris. From then on, our only outings in Paris were at night.

Aberbach and Star arranged all our reservations and took us from place to place until we were able to learn our way around. They even joined us at The Lido club for a few nights. They had a vested interest in making sure Elvis and his friends had a good time. This would be our pattern for the next 10 evenings: Watch the early show at the well-known night clubs such as Les Folies

Bergère, Moulin Rouge, Carousel, and Le Café de Paris. Later in the evening, we would catch the last show at the Lido.

Elvis was especially fond of the Lido because hardly anyone bothered him there. Occasionally someone would come over for an autograph, but for the most part we were left alone.

But what he liked most about the Lido, of course, was its girls. There were lots and lots of beautiful, voluptuous girls in the show. Surprisingly enough, all of the girls in the chorus line were from England. They were called the Blue Belles, and their home base was London. Since we didn't know French, we were thrilled they all spoke English. We were permitted to go backstage every night after the show. There the show girls all roamed about naked, without batting an eyelash. I just about fainted at this sight. Elvis and Lamar were more accustomed to this and I found out later they told the girls to give me extra attention to make me nervous. It worked. Sweat trickled from my brow every time one of them stopped to talk to me.

One night at the Lido we encountered former Olympic swimmer-turned-actress Esther Williams. Elvis put on his ol' Southern charm, calling her Miss Williams and using his best drawl. He brought her to our table and introduced us. I thought she was very gracious and lovely. She asked us how we were enjoying Paris, and added that it was her favorite city in the world.

Miss Williams' escort that evening was Bennett Cerf, a panel member on the American TV program *What's My Line?* as well as the founding publisher of Random House. He was a small, balding fellow with glasses, and I was waiting for Ms. Williams to dump him and run off with Elvis. She seemed amenable, slow dancing with Elvis as Cerf sat alone. As lovely as she was, however, Elvis was more interested in younger girls, and so returned Esther to her companion, who was a good sport about the whole thing.

For a country boy like me, raised in the hills of Tennessee, to be involved with all this brought to mind an old Southern expression: one could say that I was walking around in some pretty "tall cotton."

Every night after the revues finished, the show business people from all over Paris gathered at a place called Le Bantu, or The 4 o'clock Club, so named because it did not open until 4 a.m. We usually arrived there around 4:30 a.m. with our string of girls from the Lido. Elvis always picked out two of the best-looking ones and we were left with the rest. They were all gorgeous to us. Around 9 a.m., we left The 4 o'clock Club with several of the Blue Belle girls in tow, who accompanied us back to our hotel.

We indulged ourselves to the fullest extent in Paris, and loved every second of it. We rolled out of bed around 8 p.m. and Elvis ordered our one and only meal of the day. It was a tremendous breakfast. We had enough eggs, ham, bacon, and fresh squeezed orange juice to feed a dozen people. Included were a couple of bottles of champagne. After our feast we bathed, dressed, and primped to begin the whole routine over again.

One morning we brought back half the population of the Lido Club to our hotel. We had so many Blue Belle dancers in our suite that it created a problem.

The phone rang and Lamar answered. It was the manager of the Lido Club. He told Lamar he was ready to begin his first show of the night. Half asleep, Lamar told him, "Well, go ahead and start," and hung up the phone. A moment later the phone rang again, and it was the manager telling Lamar he wanted to start the show. Lamar slammed the phone down. A third time the phone rang and Lamar, now furious, grabbed the receiver on the first ring.

"Start the damn show!" Lamar yelled.

"But you don't understand, monsieur," the manager replied, "you have all our Blue Belle girls!" Lamar looked around the suite and realized he was right. He started rounding up all the girls, acting like their den mother. Lamar managed to fit them in four separate limousines. I figured he stuffed between seven and nine girls in each car.

When there were no girls to occupy our time, we amused ourselves in the hotel by playing with butane lighters, which had just been introduced to the market and were the hottest new toy for adults. Elvis sent Lamar, Charlie, and me out to buy some of these lighters with several cans of butane to refill them. The flame would go about two feet high with the valve control wide open.

It's a miracle we didn't burn the hotel down, trying to see who could make his flame go highest. The lighters provided fun when we were out on the town, as well, especially when we spied somebody ready with a cigarette or cigar to be lit.

"Could I give you a light, sir?"

You should have seen the expression on their faces when we presented them with two feet of flame.

Throughout our stay in Paris, Elvis unsuccessfully attempted to contact Brigitte Bardot. For some reason (as if we don't know!), he desperately wanted to meet her. Elvis got her phone number and left her several messages. But eventually he found out that she was out of the country filming a movie. Nevertheless, Elvis felt snubbed and thought she should have been there for him.

"To hell with that bitch!" he said in frustration.

Our leave passed so quickly, it was unbelievable. We were having such a great time. Our schedule called for us to catch a train back to Frankfurt the night of the 13th day. But Elvis decided that we would miss that train and stay another night. Anybody who has ever been in the Army knows that on every leave of absence there is a day of grace. As long as we made it back to Friedberg by midnight on the 15th day of our leave, we would not be considered AWOL.

Elvis hired a special limousine with driver to take us back to Germany so that we could stay in Paris an extra night. The limousine was a big, long, black Cadillac costing Elvis $800 for our trip back to our base. We arrived in Friedberg just in time to report in before midnight.

It was difficult for me to go back to soldiering, but the memories of that trip sustained me. Elvis told me afterwards that he spent $15,000 U.S. dollars on our vacation, and it was worth every penny. Of that amount, $12,800 had been spent in Paris. In 1959, that was a large sum of money. It ain't chicken feed today.

It all seems like some kind of a distant dream now. Then I was still single and free to tomcat around. But that would soon be changing.

CHAPTER FOURTEEN

Burning Love

Elisabeth

While Elvis never had the opportunity to meet his fantasy woman, Brigitte Bardot, in France, he did meet the girl of his dreams in Germany. Priscilla Beaulieu entered Elvis' life on September 13, 1959. She was brought to the house at Goethestrasse 14 to meet her idol and heartthrob by Currie Grant and his wife, Carole.

Airman First Class Currie Grant was assigned to the 497th Recon Technical Squadron at Schierstein, West Germany, near Wiesbaden on the Rhine River. His official Air Force job was filing and typing intelligence material for the Intelligence Branch. Currie also had an off-duty job in the evenings as manager of the Eagle Club in downtown Wiesbaden on Paulinenstrasse 7. The Eagle Club was the largest Air Force Club and community center in Europe. Every Saturday night Currie was the master of ceremonies and producer of a variety show held at the Eagle Club, known as the Hit Parade.

Earlier that year, Lamar, Vernon, and I attended a disabled children's benefit show in Giessen, to which Vernon donated money. It was a gala event that had such celebrities as Olivia de Havilland on the guest list. Currie Grant acted as one of the emcees for the show, and his wife Carole sang. She was from a show business family, and the sister of crooner Tony Bennett.

Currie met Lamar after the show and invited him to visit them in Wiesbaden. In return, Lamar invited the Grants to come to Bad Nauheim to meet Elvis. The Grants, along with daughters Sharon and Karen, came to Bad Nauheim a week later on a Sunday afternoon to meet Elvis.

When they arrived at Goethestrasse 14, Grandma informed them that everyone was down the street playing football. They walked to the playing field and joined Lamar and the late Cliff Gleaves, who were sitting on the sidelines watching the rest play. Cliff was an old buddy of Elvis' and had just arrived that Friday. Elvis had invited him to come to Germany when Red left. Our sympathy goes out to the family of Cliff Gleaves who passed away on Tuesday, June 4, 2002.

Cliff was an aspiring comedian, but without any notable success. He had a routine similar to that of Dave Gardner, famous nightclub entertainer from the Deep South. We enjoyed Cliff's routine and thought he was hysterical. During the introductions, Cliff heard that Currie was also in show business as an emcee and producer of a show. From that moment, Cliff latched onto Currie like a magnet.

Currie and his wife became regular Sunday visitors to the house after that first meeting.

I had only a casual relationship with the couple, but as time went on, I resented them for bringing Priscilla into Elvis' life.

Elvis allowed Currie a privilege that he did not grant even to those of us in his own inner circle. He let him take photos of him, which turned out to be a questionable decision because Currie soon began to take advantage of the situation, even though Elvis never did turn him down.

A few weeks later, Cliff moved to Wiesbaden to live with the Grants. Personally, I think Elvis resented Cliff for coming and going as he pleased. At any rate, Cliff had always been a bit more independent around Elvis than some of the others who hung around. I think Elvis kept him around because he thought Cliff was one of the funniest guys he had ever known. Cliff and Currie traveled around West Germany doing shows at various military service centers. Cliff also became a regular performer at the Eagle Club, where the two soon met another regular — Priscilla Ann Beaulieu.

Priscilla was born on May 24, 1945, in Brooklyn, New York. Her stepfather, a captain in the Air Force, had been transferred to Wiesbaden, Germany, in the middle of August. The Beaulieu family took up residence two blocks from the Eagle Club, which became a hang-out for 14-year-old Priscilla. She would go there to listen to the jukebox, watch a show, or get something to eat at the snack bar. This is where she met Grant, who agreed to introduce her to Elvis.

Currie and Carole Grant made the one-hour drive with Priscilla to the house on a Sunday night. I was busy in the kitchen with Grandma, unaware that there was company in the house. Grandma was cooking up a generous portion of bacon, and I was washing and putting away dishes.

Suddenly Elvis came running into the kitchen to get a cold drink. Obviously excited, he started raving about this girl who looked like an angel and was sitting in the living room. I noticed he had kind of a glazed-over look in his eyes indicating to me that this girl must be something special indeed.

Rex said that later that night, after Priscilla left, Elvis also told him he thought she looked like an angel. But that wasn't all.

"And she's young enough that I can train her any way I want," Elvis told Rex.

This was the first time I ever heard Elvis describe any girl with such emotion, so I decided to go to the living room and see for myself. Sure enough, she did look like an angel. She reminded me of a painting because she was flawless. She was also very petite, demure, and quiet — just what Elvis liked in a woman.

She seemed so much more sophisticated than most girls her age. Priscilla was wearing a white-and-navy sailor dress with matching white shoes. Considering the fact she had just met Elvis Presley, plus a lot of the strangers in the house, it is understandable that she seemed shy and very nervous. I assumed Priscilla and I shared something in common — she too had probably fantasized about meeting her idol, Elvis Presley, never dreaming it would actually happen. Her demeanor reminded me of the first night I met Elvis at the movie theater. It was a feeling of disbelief, shock, and excitement all rolled up into one.

It appeared to be love at first sight for Elvis. He couldn't keep his eyes off Priscilla all evening, even while playing the piano and singing to the group. Elvis was doing everything he could to impress her. He sang "Rags to Riches," "Are You Lonesome Tonight?" and "End of the Rainbow," hardly taking his eyes off her during the mini-concert.

As the evening passed, the Grants were getting more nervous with each tick of the clock. Priscilla had a curfew because she had school the next morning. She was attending the H. H. Arnold American Military High School, sponsored by the U.S. military. They would somehow have to explain her late arrival home to Captain Beaulieu.

I was accustomed to Elvis and his girlfriends, but normally these relationships were short-term. I was concerned this one might have considerable more staying power. As fate would have it, Priscilla's entering the picture altered many people's futures. In my case, it was for the better.

Elvis sent for Priscilla a few days after their initial meeting. Her parents, particularly Captain Beaulieu, were hesitant about their teenage daughter seeing the famous rock 'n' roller. Elvis coddled the Beaulieus with his "yes ma'ams" and "yes sirs," laying on his thickest charm and pulling out all the stops to placate her parents. He assured them that he would treat their daughter with total respect, and that there would always be a chaperone along when they were together. They cautiously granted permission as long as a set curfew was observed. In no time Elvis violated it, always offering a plethora of excuses.

Priscilla had a series of drivers who ferried her back and forth during the week, as well as almost every weekend starting on Friday nights. She and Elvis spent as much time as they could together, and Priscilla's grades at school suffered as a result. I imagine it wasn't easy being a ninth grader, dating the world's most famous singer, and trying to maintain a respectable grade point average.

When Priscilla came over, we all sat around in the living room, talking, laughing, and listening to music. In fact, we were putting on a show. It was the Let's Entertain Priscilla Show.

Rex, Charlie, and Lamar would sometimes sing along with Elvis as he played the piano. Other times he would use his companions, Rex mostly, as sparring partners in karate demonstrations for Priscilla. When Cliff was present, he would rehearse some of his comedy material and throw in a few impersonations. Everything was done mostly to entertain and impress Priscilla.

There were no serious conversations with Priscilla, unless it was Elvis conducting the conversation. Later in the evening, he and Priscilla would disappear upstairs in Elvis' bedroom, away from the crowd.

Meanwhile, Vernon Presley was now spending all his time with a female companion by the name of Dee Stanley, the wife of a sergeant stationed at the base.

They actually met through Elvis when he received a phone call from Dee, who offered to make him a genuine home-cooked Southern meal. She didn't know at the time that Grandma was already doing that for Elvis every single day he was in Germany.

After Elvis and Dee exchanged a few pleasantries, she forged right ahead with her agenda. Dee had a well-earned reputation for persistence. In the book *Elvis, We Love You Tender* written by Dee and her three sons, she related her attempt to appeal to his taste buds.

"Now, how would you and all your family like to have supper one night with me and my husband out here at our place?" she asked Elvis. "I'm sure you'd enjoy a little home cookin' after all that slop they feed you at the base."

"Oh, the food out there isn't so bad," Elvis replied, obviously stalling for time to think of a way to politely decline the unsolicited invitation. He continued, "Well, thank you very much for the invitation, ma'am. It's sweet of you to think of us, but I have to go on maneuvers next week. Why don't you call back this Monday, and I'll speak to my daddy about it?"

Elvis suggested they meet at the Grunewald for coffee when Dee called back on the appointed day. Elvis never intended to meet her, and sent his father in his place. I'm sure he never imagined that the meeting would begin a relationship that would end up in marriage.

Dee arrived at the Grunewald in a black outfit with matching black shoes. She was dressed to impress. Vernon had been waiting, and called her name out when he noticed her. They got along famously right away. She found him very handsome and charming, while he was just as attracted to her. Vernon called Dee the very next day to set up another date. This time the meeting would include Dee's husband, Bill.

Bill Stanley had once been General George Patton's personal bodyguard. The Stanleys, along with their three boys, were living in Germany. Vernon started spending his spare time with Dee and Bill. The three of them became good friends.

The trio frequented the American military clubs on base. Vernon usually left at evening time, but returned later after everyone else had gone to bed. Some mornings he would show up at breakfast with dark circles under his eyes and suffering from a serious hangover. Elvis must have noticed his father's condition, but respected Vernon too much to bring it up. Never did I hear him say a word out of line to his dad.

As Vernon continued to spend time with Dee and Sergeant Bill Stanley, the dynamic changed. It wasn't long before three became a crowd.

The Stanleys' marriage deteriorated, and they separated. Vernon and Dee quietly began dating each other. Dee's three young sons were sent to live with her sister in Norfolk, Virginia, until Dee returned to the States. In the meantime, Vernon acted like he was madly in love with Dee, and a week later, she moved into the house. Elvis was not thrilled when they played the role of honeymooners in front of him.

"Burnt," Elvis muttered. In the Presleys' private language, his father was hurting his feelings. Though he never went beyond that, Elvis' reaction made it plain to Vernon that his father's behavior wounded him.

As painful as all this was for Elvis, he never openly criticized his father in front of anyone. They had grown especially close since Gladys' death. Elvis always acted polite and gracious towards Dee, even though it must have been difficult for him.

After Dee moved in, Elvis and Vernon instructed me to tell Frau Pieper that Dee and Vernon were secretly married. In addition, I was to inform her it was extremely important to keep the marriage a total secret outside the house. Elvis and Vernon knew the press would have a field day with Vernon's scandalous affair. They also knew Colonel Parker would go ballistic if anything came out in the papers about it.

Dee was an attractive blonde in her early thirties, and was usually dressed to the hilt. Her perfume left a trail, so it was always easy to detect when she was in the house.

From what Elvis and Grandma said, Dee was the complete opposite of Gladys, and those of us within the inner group could sense that Elvis was not pleased about the situation. I think he expected his dad to be in mourning over Gladys for a longer period of time, and he could not accept his dad having a serious relationship with another woman.

Grandma was more openly critical, especially with me, about Dee and Vernon. She felt that Dee was leaving her husband and shelving her kids because Vernon was the father of a famous celebrity and had money. "That woman is nothing but a gold digger, among other things," Grandma said to me.

It wasn't long before Dee started invading Grandma's turf, coming in the kitchen to help cook. She would offer to make homemade biscuits, and her recipe differed from Grandma's — a double mortal sin. I will say Dee's biscuits were as tasty as Grandma's, but somehow I never got around to mentioning it to Grandma. After Dee left the kitchen, Grandma dished out the dirt. She commented on the flashy way Dee dressed every day and made disparaging remarks about her cooking.

"Her biscuits are better suited to play baseball with than to eat," Grandma quipped. Dee soon learned that the kitchen was Grandma's territory. Anyone in the house could sense the tension between these two women. Next to Dee, Frau Pieper was almost Grandma's kissing cousin.

Every three or four months, Grandma had me write letters to her two daughters. She would tell them about her daily routine, Elvis' life in the Army, Vernon's duties while in Germany, and how glad she was that I was there to keep her company. She never mentioned anything about Dee Stanley in any of her letters. I guess she was hoping the relationship with Vernon would pass.

Dee must not have cared for the way Grandma cooked for the Presley men, because she and Vernon frequently went out for dinner, and then stayed out until it was time to go to bed. I don't recall seeing them in the living room, visiting with the rest of our group. They were very independent, and spent much of their time alone. Also, they were older. We didn't fit in with them and vice versa. I often wondered if Dee wanted to keep a low profile because she was still married. They must have known their relationship made Elvis uncomfortable.

Dee was kind to me from the get-go. Since she knew my real feelings for Elvis, she tried to help me win him over. For example, she helped me with my makeup and showed me new hairstyles, or gave me girl-to-girl advice on how to handle myself. Occasionally, Dee and Vernon invited me to dinner. This was especially helpful when another girl was in the house with Elvis. I genuinely appreciated her concern on my behalf. I assumed it was her idea to encourage Vernon to take me along with them to make up for the time I lost with Elvis when he was with Priscilla so much.

One evening the three of us went to a party together where there was a lot of drinking taking place. Elvis never allowed alcohol in the house, so Vernon had to drink outside of the home. Since he usually came home after everyone else had gone to bed, no one would know of his drunken condition. It turned out that Vernon had too much that evening and got into an argument with Dee. I made the mistake of siding with Dee and Vernon slapped me in the face because I disagreed with him. Dee got very mad at Vernon, and made him apologize to me immediately. The following day, a sober, contrite Vernon apologized to me again in private. He said the alcohol took over, and he behaved badly.

"Please don't tell Elvis," Vernon begged. He knew Elvis would be furious at him for striking me. That was one thing about Elvis — he treated all his girls with that "Love Me Tender" respect. I kept my promise to Vernon and never told Elvis about that night. It was never mentioned again by Vernon, Dee, or myself.

With Elvis falling so hard for Priscilla, and Vernon so smitten with Dee, love was blooming at Goethestrasse 14. But not just for the Presleys.

CHAPTER FIFTEEN

Suspicious Minds

Rex

Almost a year passed since I had brought Elisabeth down the aisle of the Tower Theater in Grafenwohr to meet Elvis. Up to this point, Elisabeth and I had no personal contact and our conversation was minimal, just small talk. Eye contact was not permitted by Elvis. Like a good soldier following an order, I carried out Elvis' wishes to the max.

It was Grandma who was responsible for getting me to break ranks where Elisabeth was concerned.

The more girls there were for Elvis, the more time Elisabeth spent with Grandma. Female companionship came and went in the Presley household and Grandma mostly turned a blind eye to it all. However, it didn't mean she was oblivious to what was going on. Because Elisabeth and I were special in Grandma's life, she decided that we would make a good couple.

In my opinion, there were two main reasons why Elisabeth became interested in me. First, Elisabeth finally admitted to herself that Elvis wasn't exactly a one-woman man. Second, Grandma sensed Elisabeth's heartache and wanted to help her get over Elvis. She figured if Elisabeth fell in love with someone else, it would take her mind off her grandson. "That Rex Mansfield is such a nice young man, and he'll make some girl a good husband," Grandma told Elisabeth.

Out of the group of guys that frequently visited the house, I was the only one to pay much attention to Grandma. I sincerely liked Grandma and enjoyed spending time talking with her because we shared similar backgrounds. She was a simple country girl and I was a country boy. We discussed things like growing up on farms, raising animals, and growing vegetables and crops. We also shared a Southern Baptist upbringing. She reminded me of my maternal grandmother, Mammy Roberts: both were tall, slender and frail, both were worn hard from years of back-breaking labor on the farm. They were in the prime of their lives during the Great Depression of the 1930s, and there was nothing to do but work your butt off to survive.

It was in early October, 1959, when Grandma first put the bug in my ear concerning Elisabeth. In the beginning she spoke to us separately about each other, and this went on for some time.

"Rex, you know that Elisabeth is sure a sweet person, and she'll make some man a good wife," Grandma would tell me, same as she told Elisabeth about me.

We both listened to what Grandma was saying, but at first neither took any action on the matter. Frankly, I didn't even want to entertain romantic thoughts about Elisabeth for fear of reper-cussions on the Elvis front. Grandma never gave up, and eventually took matters directly into hand. One time when Elvis left the house, she had us both in her room together, telling us what she thought. Grandma had more nerve than Elisabeth and I put together. Had Elvis found out what Grandma was up to, she would be sent packing for Memphis, Elisabeth would have gone back to Grafenwohr, and I would be banished from the inner circle for good.

In spite of myself, slowly but surely I began to look at Elisabeth in a different light. Initially, I only allowed myself to have short daydreams of her. In the back of my mind, I was worried that a beautiful girl like Elisabeth would never fall for me. But perhaps Elisabeth would realize her chances with Elvis were slim, and she would entertain the thought of seeing me.

This situation proved nerve-racking for both of us. It was like playing Russian roulette, walking in a mine field and skating on thin ice, all at the same time.

Finally, Elisabeth and I decided to take the final step and began making plans for a secret date.

Enter Rod and Vee Harris. Rod was a career Army man and the mechanic responsible for Elvis' jeep. His and Elvis' professional relationship in the field blossomed into a personal friendship when they were off-duty, and Rod and his wife, Vee, became regular visitors at the house. Vee even helped Elisabeth with the fan mail, and the two became fast friends. Eventually Elisabeth confided in Vee her frustrations with Elvis and her interest in me.

Vee sympathized with Elisabeth's situation. She recognized the double standard Elvis set, and knew Elisabeth was being strung along. "Maybe you can come to our house and meet up with Rex," Vee suggested to Elisabeth.

Since we could never risk going out in public for fear of it being reported back to Elvis, this was the perfect arrangement. On a Saturday night, the wheels were set in motion. We had to be extremely careful around Elvis. Even though there were plenty of girls and guys around constantly, Elvis always seemed able to keep track of everyone.

One night, Elisabeth told Elvis she was going over to visit with Rod and Vee. I covered my own tracks by telling Elvis I was on duty. I had to be sure that Elvis would have no reason to miss me or ask where I was, and we both had to make sure our plans to meet would not conflict with any plans Elvis made for the group. It was our luck that he intended to spend a quiet night at the house alone with Priscilla.

Elisabeth was the first to arrive at the Harris household, and I got there shortly thereafter. Rod and Vee were kind enough to escort us to their living room, then excused themselves and shut the door behind them.

"Have fun kids," they said in unison. "Make yourselves at home and stay as long as you dare." I'd like to say we demurely talked each other's ears off, but the fact is there wasn't much talking going on, mostly a whole lot of smooching and embracing.

You belong in my arms forever, I thought. It was a very unusual situation. Elisabeth was hungry for affection from a man, and my desire for her was both sudden and beyond my comprehension. When the two of us finally got together, the sparks flew and the fire was ignited. Neither of us held back, believing our love was meant to be.

We managed to see each other about twice a week, always at the Harris' house. The more time Elisabeth and I spent together, the stronger our relationship became. Elisabeth would call me to let me know when Elvis was tied up. Priscilla was occupying more and more of his time, which gave us the perfect window of opportunity.

Something else working in our favor was Dee Stanley. Vernon was so wrapped up in his romance with her that he didn't notice Elisabeth and I were having an affair. Even now it sounds bizarre to call it that, since we were both single adults; but under the circumstances that's what it was. Usually Vernon was very inquisitive and paid careful attention to what Elvis' inner circle of friends did, but now his attention was solely on Dee. Had Vernon found us out, I'm sure he would have immediately gone to Elvis with the news. Unfortunately for us, not everybody in the house had his head in the clouds.

Eventually Lamar began noticing that whenever Elisabeth left the house, I was nowhere to be found. He put two and two together and figured out we were seeing each other. Lamar mentioned his hunch to Elisabeth, and assured her he would never spill the beans to Elvis. Elisabeth never confirmed it to Lamar, but he seemed pretty sure of himself. Cliff also found out, most likely from Lamar. They were very close and always supported each other when Elvis got upset with one or the other. Their natural affection and loyalty for Elvis notwithstanding, they remained tight-lipped.

Elisabeth, however, had several other close calls. Elvis constantly asked her where she had been and who she had seen. Her stock answer was that she had been to Rod and Vee's house for a visit, which satisfied him.

One incident was too close for comfort. Elisabeth and I got carried away on our date, and didn't notice how much time had passed. Elvis had imposed a midnight curfew on her, and with Priscilla gone by then and Elisabeth nowhere to be found, he was getting twitchy.

Frantic, Elvis called the Harris' home. In trying to cover for us, they reacted with detectable nervousness that only aroused Elvis' suspicions. But Rod and Vee did enough damage control to put him off our scent.

Back at the Presley household, Elvis turned his anger on Lamar.

"Lamar, you'd better tell me who she's with," Elvis threatened. "Is she seeing another guy? I'll ship your fat ass back home if you don't tell me the truth."

At times, Lamar would get testy and talk back to Elvis. This was one of those times. "Hell Elvis, can you blame her if she is seeing someone?" Lamar shot back. "The way you treat her, how in the hell could you blame her for seeing someone else? I certainly don't blame her, and I hope she had some fun for a change." Lamar's unexpected nerve sent Elvis reeling, and he turned on his heel to retreat to his bedroom.

A few minutes later Elisabeth was knocking on the front door. Luckily, Lamar answered and let Elisabeth know what had transpired. "Be very careful what you say to Elvis because he suspects something's going on," Lamar warned her. "For God's sake, don't tell him you were with Rex if you want to continue having a relationship with him and stay here, too."

Just then, Elvis came barreling down the stairs to confront Elisabeth. "Elisabeth, why are you nearly two hours past curfew? Tell me the truth honey, are you seeing somebody else?" he asked.

"Elvis, I've had a very long night," Elisabeth said. "Can we talk about this in the morning? I promise to tell you all about it." Her answer caught Elvis off guard, and he didn't press the issue then. But she had no doubt that by morning he was going to grill her like a frothing prosecutor in search of a conviction.

Why couldn't Elisabeth just go ahead and tell Elvis that she liked me very much and wanted to date me? Why did she have to continue to see me secretly? The truth was, Elisabeth was trying the timeless game of wanting to have her cake and eat it, too. I might have been wanting my cake, too — access to Elvis and a forbidden romance with his secretary — but make no mistake, I would have dropped my friendship with Elvis in a heartbeat to be with Elisabeth.

She was interested in me, but still wanted to be with Elvis. At this point, my jealousy was starting to work overtime. The fact that she went home to Elvis every night compounded the problem — so much so that it took years for me to overcome that jealousy and the deep anger that built up during that time. I guess that was the price I had to pay for courting a beautiful woman Elvis Presley also found equally desirable.

I felt I offered Elisabeth something that she couldn't ever have with Elvis — commitment, true love, and affection. Elvis was only hers part of the time — and once Priscilla came into the picture, that time was increasingly less. Elisabeth thought Elvis would throw her out if he uncovered the truth about us, and she wasn't ready to give up even a small part of Elvis for me. I had no such qualms about risking my friendship to the man.

I'm not really sure why I started dating Elisabeth behind Elvis' back. I suspect Grandma was the first reason, since she put the notion into my head. Later, maybe it was the intrigue of the situation. Perhaps it was also the natural ongoing competition between Elvis and me. It could have been the simple fact that Grandma believed it should be this way. Probably it was the combination of all these elements. In any case, once we started dating, I truly fell in love with Elisabeth and I couldn't help myself. I knew it was wrong to do this behind a friend's back. I realized I was afraid that Elvis would make an example of me to the other guys if I confessed. The whole affair — there's that word again — was the most stressful experience of my entire life.

Here I was — a normal, ordinary, everyday sort of guy, trying to take a girl away from one of the most famous and sought-after men in the world. Who did I think I was, anyway? I confided in my close friend, John La Fatta, whom I met in Germany. He was an independent, rugged individual who was not impressed with Elvis (whom he also knew), his fame, or his fancy lifestyle. He was sick of seeing Elisabeth being used by Elvis. "Rex, why don't you tell Elvis that Elisabeth is dating me," John suggested. "I don't care about my friendship with him anyway."

I was touched that John would go out on a limb for Elisabeth and me. He cared more for me than his relationship with Elvis. That was quite an honor considering nearly everybody on base begged to be Elvis' friend. Having Elvis Presley as your friend brought with it many privileges, not the least of which was a sort of second-hand celebrity for yourself.

Once John offered to do this for me, I called Lamar with the news. He thought the idea was superb, and passed it on to Elisabeth. Elvis was still waiting for an answer, and now she had one. She told him she had gone on only one date with John, and they weren't even alone. I think Elvis calmed down when she promised never to see him again. I was relieved it got us both off the hook, at least for the time being. John ceased all visits to the house after this, which suited him just fine. He was not the type to kiss up or bow down to anyone. John was one of a handful of people who supported our secret affair.

One night, Lamar, Cliff, and I went over to the Park Hotel for coffee and discussed the secret relationship. Lamar and Cliff agreed that it was fantastic because this was the first time anybody had dared to take a girl away from Elvis. They had fun with the scenario. "Nobody's ever dared to do this before," Lamar said excitedly, snapping his fingers. "Elvis needs a little payback every now and then for some of the stunts he pulls."

They also seemed somewhat amused at the whole drama unfolding and strongly advised against telling Elvis anything. Maybe it was their way of getting back at Elvis for some of the things Elvis had done to them. They reminded me that in the past they had brought girlfriends around Elvis, and if the mood struck him and Elvis fancied their girls, he would take them for himself.

I actually saw this happen once to Lamar. I'll never forget the look of pain that came across his face as he watched Elvis and his girl go upstairs. When Elvis was out of earshot, Lamar yelled out "Burnt!" several times. He threw in some curse words that left no doubt about his pain and frustration. It was quite an embarrassing moment, and also a revealing one.

I, on the other hand, felt terrible for him. With Elvis and his girls, it was a one-way street. Blame it on his ego, but one thing was for sure — nobody was allowed to touch what he considered his private property. Elvis didn't like competition with his girls, his career, or even the Army except when he could control things — including the outcome.

Elvis' competitive nature even reared its ugly head with me after the Army promoted me to Sergeant E-5 on December 1, 1959. The promotion board was made up of our battalion commander, a colonel, one executive officer who was a major and our five company commanders, who were all captains.

I had never faced that much brass before with me as the center of their attention. They ordered me to meet them in the command headquarters building in the second floor room where they held strategy meetings. I was directed to a single chair in the middle of the room, facing my superiors seated behind a long table. I wore my dress-greens uniform as I marched into the room, snapping my heels together and saluting them with my eyes straight ahead, shoulders back, chest out, practically shouting my arrival. "Acting Sergeant Donald R. Mansfield, U.S. 25255673 reporting as ordered, sirs." It was an impressive entrance if I do say so myself.

Each of the promotion board officers took his time peppering me with questions about the Army, my job, my tank company, current events, and possible battlefield situations. After an hour of constant, intense, and sometimes intimidating questions, they unanimously cast their vote for me to be promoted to Sergeant E-5. They also recommended that I apply for Officer Candidate School because they felt I had a real future in the Army, but I told them that I had a good civilian job waiting for me back in the States.

Lamar, ever the one-upsman, got a big kick out of my promotion because I had made Sergeant before Elvis. He warned me to be careful how I talked about the promotion in front of Elvis because he was jealous I got promoted before him.

I was very proud of my promotion and despite Lamar's warning, went straight to Elvis to show him my promotion papers. The stripes on my arm would be for real, not simply "acting." It was the only time during my two years with Elvis that I ever asked him to take a picture with me. He readily agreed and congratulated me on my promotion, but the picture taken that day tells the true tale of how Elvis felt. In it, his trademark smile was noticeably absent. But Elvis once again cast himself as the hero of the promotion.

"I'll be making Sergeant in a few days, and, Rex, you know if it hadn't been for me, you would not have ever made Sergeant,"

Elvis insisted. He went on to say that if he had been the only one of the original group from Tennessee to make Sergeant, the world would say that he was being shown favoritism.

"Rexadus, see what good things can happen to you just because you know me," Elvis boasted.

I absolutely resented his comments, especially since he'd gone out of his way to make them in front of the group. Elvis may have actually believed this bull himself, but no one else did. In fact, we all joked about it later, when Elvis wasn't around. I was relieved the guys didn't give his fable any credence.

When we were on maneuvers in the Black Forest, near the Swiss border, Elvis got his own promotion — about eight weeks later, on January 20, 1960. He was so proud of those stripes, and rightly so. Not many men go into the Army during peacetime as a private E-1 and come out of the Army two years later as Sergeant E-5. I was genuinely thrilled for him, and helped him remove his old Specialist E-4 stripes.

While his promotion took a tremendous amount of pressure off me, my real-life situation with Elisabeth was beginning to mirror a plot of a Hollywood movie. Coincidentally, right around then, Elvis gave me the opportunity to visit an actual movie set.

The film *G.I. Blues* started shooting exteriors and Army footage while he was still in the Army. In October 1959, movie producer Hal Wallis came to Bad Nauheim. Elvis had movie and record contracts that were still in effect while he was in the Army. Elvis was glad to share the details with me, and freely admitted that Colonel Parker was the real negotiator. His film contract provided that he receive 50 percent of the gross income, plus $250,000 U.S. dollars in advance for signing the contract, and $100,000 for expenses while the movie was being filmed. I was blown away by these figures.

Elvis had already made *Love Me Tender, Loving You, Jailhouse Rock,* and *King Creole* before being drafted into the Army. Colonel Parker had signed four or five more movie deals to commence as soon as Elvis was discharged.

Elvis took me on location one day and we watched some of the tank battles being filmed. He could not participate in the filming personally until after he left the Army. I am not sure if that was the Army's rule or Colonel Parker's. The Army did supply the tanks and the training area to shoot the scenes. This was good publicity for the military. As things got underway, a search was started for a GI who could serve as Elvis' stand-in. About 50 GI's tried out from various Kasernes in the area, and one guy was finally picked who the movie folks thought looked the most like Elvis. The one they chose really didn't look at all like Elvis up close, but from a distance, with some careful camera angles, he could pass.

Elvis' recording contract with RCA at that time called for a cool $1,000 per week, guaranteed for 20 years, plus five cents for each record sold. The percentage on albums would be the same as or equal to the five cents for singles. That was not exactly chump change. Elvis' singles had sold over 54 million copies by 1958. Fifty-four million times five cents per copy equals $2.7 million, and that was a pile of money back in 1958. This seems incredible to me even today.

Elvis showed me a check from RCA which had been mailed erroneously to Bad Nauheim. The check was for $279,000, and represented royalties earned on record sales for a period of just three months. Elvis returned the check to RCA for deposit in his trust fund, which was set up to minimize any tax obligation by spreading his income out, rather than paying all at once. I was fascinated and a bit awed with the whole money thing.

A guy could flutter a lot of female hearts with a bank balance like Elvis'. I couldn't compete with him on that level, but I already had a leg up on one of Elvis' gals, and that was better than money in the bank.

CHAPTER SIXTEEN

G.I. Blues

Rex

Living with Elvis was not unlike staying at a hotel — some of the other guests were polite and well-behaved, and some were just plain crazy. There was this health nut from Johannesburg, South Africa, who called himself Dr. Laurenz Landau. He posed as a dermatologist who had created a magic formula to prevent aging. The good doctor claimed that he himself was actually in his late nineties.

In October 1959, Landau sent Elvis a letter explaining how he had helped other celebrities discover the fountain of youth. Elvis was always a sucker for a pretty face, chiefly his own. Landau enclosed photographs of himself with other famous stars, and had "legitimate" references backing his bold claims. His program, which he called Aroma Therapy Treatments, con-sisted of nothing more than an "elixir" of flowers, yogurt, and resins. "Elvis," he wrote, "after 10 weeks of receiving my treat-ments you will notice a big difference. Your acne scars will disappear, future wrinkles will be prevented, and your pores will be minimized."

Elvis had Elisabeth get in touch with Landau right away. On November 27, he showed up at the house with baggage and health treatment kits ready. He stayed in one of the local hotels and came to the house every evening to smear this miracle gunk on Elvis' face. These three-hour sessions took place in Elvis' bedroom.

Landau would pack Elvis' face with a black mud compound and leave it on for about one hour. Then he would take it off, only to apply a different compound on his face for another hour. He would repeat this process a third time with an additional face mask. Elvis wouldn't dream of letting any of us see him in this condition. One evening, however, curiosity got the better of Elisabeth. She snuck in his bedroom for a glimpse of this bizarre ritual. She told us Elvis looked like a freak.

In addition to the treatments, Landau would leave all kinds of health foods along with a large variety of vitamins and health pills. At least 25 different pills were to be taken at intervals. Elisabeth had to write the order down for Elvis, according to pill color, so he would know when to take what. This went on every day for three weeks.

Elvis never revealed to us how much he paid for these treatments and only he and Vernon knew for sure; but we heard from other sources that Elvis forked over as much as $15,000.

A week before Christmas, Landau persuaded Elvis to let him give a full body massage along with his usual facial treatment. What Landau was interested in was letting his fingers do the walking. Next thing Elvis knew, the doc had his hand on the King's family jewels. Elvis' shrill shriek resounded throughout the house. He came rushing down the stairs from his bedroom, cursing like the devil. "I'm going to kill the son of a bitch! I'm going to kill the son of a bitch!" Elvis yelled repeatedly.

In between the profanities he muttered something like, "the bastard is a queer." Lamar restrained Elvis from attacking Landau, letting the rest of the guys do the dirty work. They grabbed Landau and dragged him out the front door, through the front gate, and unceremoniously tossed him and his medical "bag of tricks" out on the street.

Acting as if nothing happened, Landau dropped by a few days before Christmas as if he was visiting old pals. He held out his hand and wished everybody a Merry Christmas. What he did next was a stunner. He looked at Elvis and asked:

"So Elvis, when would you like your next appointment?" Elvis went bonkers and told him to get the hell out. This time Landau matched him decibel for decibel. He claimed he had all sorts of damning evidence, such as tape recordings and pictures of Elvis with a young female in a compromising position. Landau threatened to go public with them unless Elvis paid him in full for the agreed-upon 10 weeks of treatments. Surprisingly, Elvis acceded to avoid any negative publicity and gave Landau a few hundred dollars for the treatments, and a one-way ticket to London. A situation like this, Elvis already knew was a no-win situation.

But since there was attempted blackmail involved, Elvis was forced to tell the Provost Marshal's Office everything that occurred. The Military Police then escorted Landau all the way back to South Africa, and Elvis never heard from this quack again. The matter even caught the attention of J. Edgar Hoover, the director of the Federal Bureau of Investigation, who documented the incident and kept it in Elvis' permanent file.

Elvis wanted to forget the whole incident and focus on the holidays. He asked me to spend my time off for Christmas of 1959 at his home in Bad Nauheim. He also gave me permission to telephone my parents, which I greatly appreciated. My phone call made the front page of the *Dresden Enterprise*, our local weekly newspaper. The headline over the story read, "Rex Mansfield spends Christmas with Elvis Presley, and calls his parents from Presley's German residence." This was the second time I graced the front page thanks to my relationship with Elvis.

Elvis had hoped that he would be able to get a discharge from the Army by Christmas because of a good conduct dispensation. The thought of spending the holiday at Graceland had Elvis very excited, but it was not to be. For whatever reasons, his discharge was delayed until March of 1960, which put Elvis into a deep funk.

A few weeks after he received the bad news and a few days before Christmas, a large package was delivered to Goethestrasse 14. Elvis had no choice but to be suspicious of anything in the mail that was out of the ordinary, especially a large package like this one. It was a huge pine box, postmarked from the United States with no return address. There are a lot of freaky people out there who send very weird stuff to celebrities, and Elvis backed away from the box like it might explode any second.

He told us to take it into another room and find out what was inside. We were quite surprised to find it was a good old-fashioned Christmas tree, with the pine needles still intact. It must have been sprayed with some kind of preservative. Not only that, it was fully decorated with stringed popcorn, ornaments, and a mistletoe on top!

"What in the hell is this?" Elvis said with a wide-open grin when he stepped into the room. He was clearly blown away by the thoughtfulness of the fan who wanted Elvis to have a traditional American Christmas.

"Ain't that something!" Elvis said, actually getting misty-eyed over it. "I've got the most loyal fans in all the world." The Christmas tree clearly made his holiday. He had us set it up in a corner of the house and we placed several gifts under it.

That tree infused Elvis with the Christmas spirit. He donated $1,500 to a nearby orphanage called Landesjugendenheim Steinmuehle, run by Hermann Schaub. The donation allowed Schaub to buy presents for all 115 children who lived at the orphanage. Of course, Elvis requested that his donation be kept under wraps, but Schaub was so overwhelmed by Elvis' generosity that he publicly thanked him, saying that while he didn't understand his music, he thought he was a terrific human being. "Never in the history of the orphanage has anyone treated the children so well," Schaub told a reporter.

On Christmas Day, Elvis hosted a huge party for family, friends, and his fellow soldiers. Everyone was having a great time and really enjoying himself. There was romance in the air — at least for those who could afford to strut their stuff. That obviously included Vernon and Dee, and it also included Elvis after Vernon and Dee picked up Priscilla at her home and brought her to the party. When Elvis saw Priscilla in her print dress with a high collar, he lit up brighter than the Christmas tree. He instantly became oblivious to all the other girls at the party.

"Cilla!" he called out as soon as she walked through the door. "You're the prettiest girl in the room."

I thought that a bit on the insensitive side. Furthermore, Elvis was wrong since Elisabeth clearly held that honor. Seeing her across the room, but not being able to reach out and touch her or kiss her under the mistletoe was torture, but we both knew the rules.

My public isolation from Elisabeth wasn't the only thing eating at me. There was also a tremendous amount of guilt building up inside of me. I was in Elvis' home, accepting his hospitality, and sneaking around behind his back dating one of his girls. For the first time since Elisabeth and I became an item, I felt like a hypocrite.

In the beginning, it had all been so exciting. Dating Elisabeth held enjoyment of forbidden fruit. Only now it was beginning to sour on me and I felt guilty. I began telling myself, You can't win over Elisabeth and you're going to lose a famous friend in the process. Rex, old buddy, is it worth it?

I popped a few extra amphetamines to dull the pain. I was now up to three pills a day, but since I was depressed I took a few more than usual. They did not have an immediate effect. I noticed Elvis and Priscilla in the corner of the living room exchanging gifts. He presented her with a small wrapped box. When she opened it her eyes got huge and she squealed with delight. "Elvis, I'll cherish these forever," she promised. He was just as excited to give the gift as she was to receive it.

Then as usual, Elvis wanted to do a little bragging, so he walked Priscilla around the room and made her show everyone her new jewelry — it was a beautiful gold watch and a ring inlaid with a pearl, surrounded by two diamonds. When I saw it, it just about sent me right back to my vial of pills. I couldn't even tell Elisabeth I loved her, much less shower her with expensive baubles.

After Priscilla finished showing off her jewelry, it was her turn to give Elvis his Christmas gift from her. It turned out to be a pair of bongos inlaid with brass.

"Bongos! Just what I always wanted," Elvis laughed aloud. Priscilla would later discover he already had a closet full of bongos.

Apparently inspired by the musical instrument, Elvis moved over to the piano to entertain his guests, although of course that was secondary to impressing Priscilla. She snuggled close to him on the piano bench while he played and sang "I'll Be Home for Christmas."

Around 3 a.m., everybody cleared out. Elvis said goodbye to his guests, wished them a Merry Christmas, and gave Priscilla a special good night kiss.

Whatever holiday spirit I had left went out of me with a whoosh not long after that, as Elvis turned to me and patted me on the back.

"Well, Rexadus old buddy, I guess it's time to say good night," he said. He wished me a final Merry Christmas and instructed me to make myself at home.

He then took Elisabeth's hand and led her upstairs into his bedroom. I stood there feeling as if my heart had been ripped from my chest. I never felt so alone in my entire life.

Then I did the only thing I could think of, the only thing I thought could take away the pain of watching my world crash down around me. I took a few more pills. I was downstairs in the living room, and the now silent night made me feel even lonelier. Waiting for the goofballs to kick in, I thought listening to a record might lift my spirits. I reached for the first album I could find, not paying attention to what it was. As I placed it on the record player, I noticed it was by one of Elvis' favorites, the Harmonizing Four. The song, titled "All Things Are Possible," reached out to me. I had heard it many times before, but tonight it sounded different. The lyrics seemed to be appealing to me personally.

> *Only believe, my brother, only believe.*
> *All things are possible if you only believe.*
> *My brother, only believe, yes brother,*
> *All things are possible if you only believe.*

I met God one morning, my soul feeling so bad.
Life's heavy burden I came by down here.
He lifted all my burdens, right now I'm feeling glad.
All things are possible, if you only believe.

I thought I was in an impossible predicament. I was in love with a girl that belonged to a close friend. The close friend happened to be rich, handsome, and very famous. I wasn't ready for Elvis to know about us. I was concerned about the consequences and not prepared to deal with them. Besides, I wasn't even 100 percent sure that Elisabeth would come with me if I did tell Elvis about us. Look where she was right now.

The amphetamines finally began to catch up, and my mind began a torturous journey illuminated by drug-induced hallucinations. I was so hopped-up I imagined seeing wavy, crawling things on the walls. They looked like worms, and they appeared everywhere. I wanted to start running and screaming my head off.

What saved me that night was the song by the Harmonizing Four. Like so many people in this world, I only turned to God when things became unbearable. It had ministered to my heart in ways I would only understand much later in life. I went to God on my knees in prayer right there in that living room, and He brought me through a night of hell on earth. For the first and last time (thank God) in my life, I was happy to see the day after Christmas, and felt relieved to be back at my barracks.

New Year's Eve went better. I recall staying up all night and toasting the arrival of 1960. But the celebrating wasn't over yet, because Elvis' 25th birthday was January 8. He received a telephone call from Dick Clark in honor of the occasion. The interview was played on the popular television show *American Bandstand*. Clark

On Family Day at Ray Barracks, Elvis is in the driver's compartment of a tank, while his dad, Vernon, stands in the tank. Elisabeth is next to Vernon, and Kathy, a part-time secretary, is next to Elisabeth. (courtesy of U.S. Army)

Elvis stands beside his jeep at Friedberg Ray Barracks.

Elvis drinks out of a cup at Ray Barracks.

Standing in front of the Hotel Prince de Galles are: Rex, Charlie, Lamar (with his back turned behind Charlie), Elvis, and men with Hill and Range Music, London (courtesy of Erik Ent. Copyright 1968)

Elvis in center in uniform with the others walking down a street in Paris (Rex at far right) (courtesy of Erik Ent. Copyright 1968)

Charlie, Rex, Lamar, Hill and Range owner, and Elvis at Lido in Paris. (with Charlie's autograph)

Charlie, Hill and Range owners, Lamar, Rex (behind Elvis), and Elvis have champagne at Lido.

Elvis with male ice skater who is part of a father-daughter team at Lido

Female ice skater who performs with her father at Lido takes a picture with Elvis.

Rex stands in front of his tank.

Rex works on C.Q.
(Charge of Quarters)

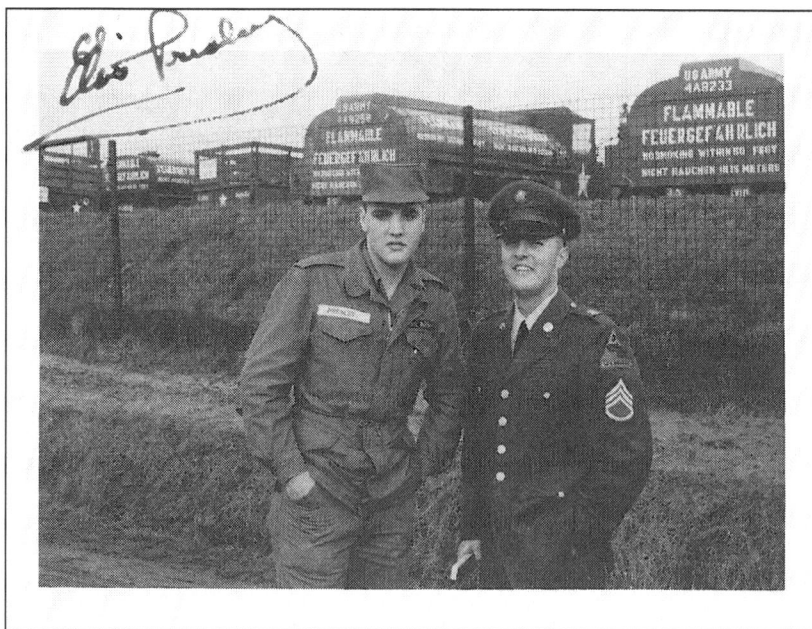

Autographed photo of Rex with Elvis when Rex made Sergeant

Shortly after he made Sergeant, Rex sent this photo of himself to his mother.

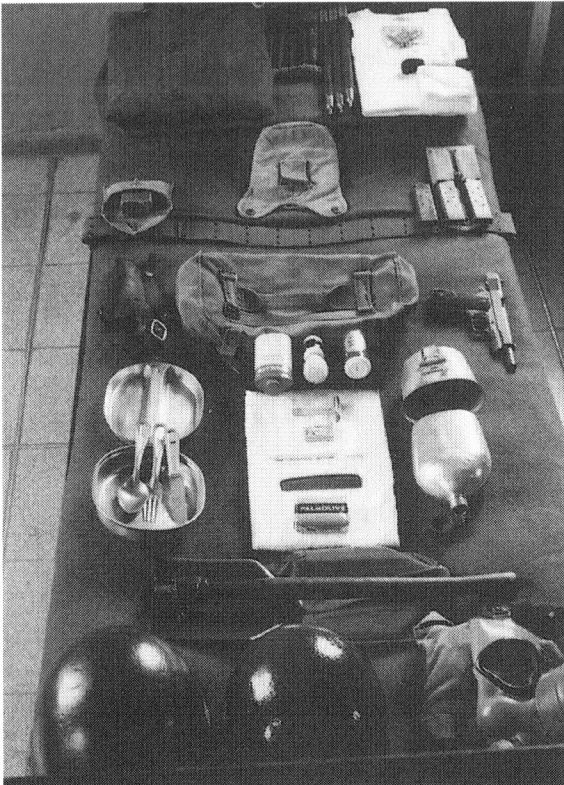

Rex's full field kit laid out on his bunk for inspection

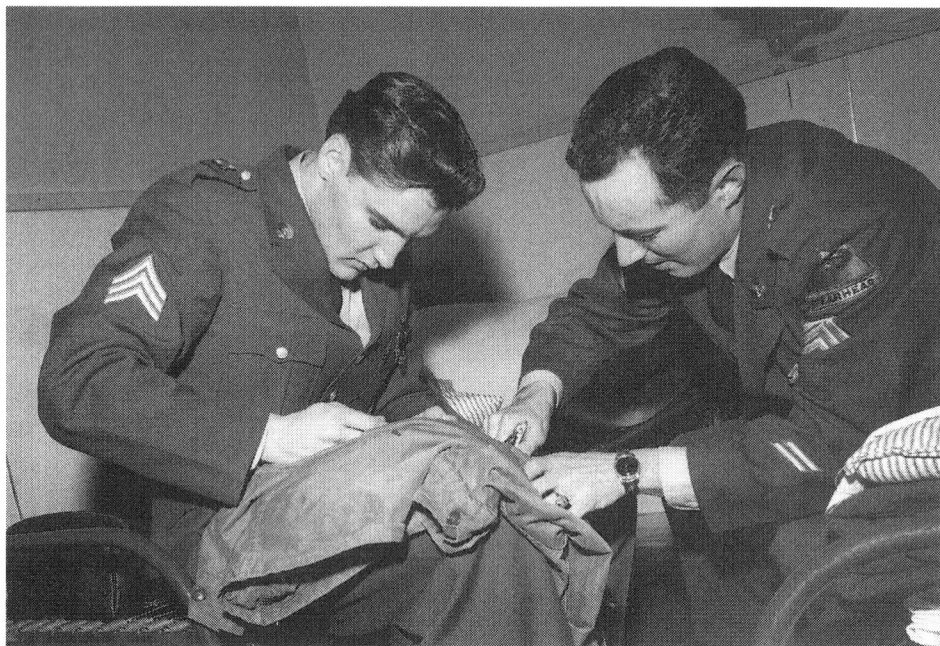

This photo shows Elvis and Rex when Elvis made Sergeant. Rex helps Elvis take off his old Specialist E-4 insignia.

Elvis after he made Sergeant (sitting down)

Elvis after making Sergeant

Elvis wears his sergeant stripes.

Elvis and Rex have their last meal together at the U.S. Army's expense.

Elvis, Rex, and Nathaniel Wigginson in formation in the snow at Fort Dix during processing out of the Army

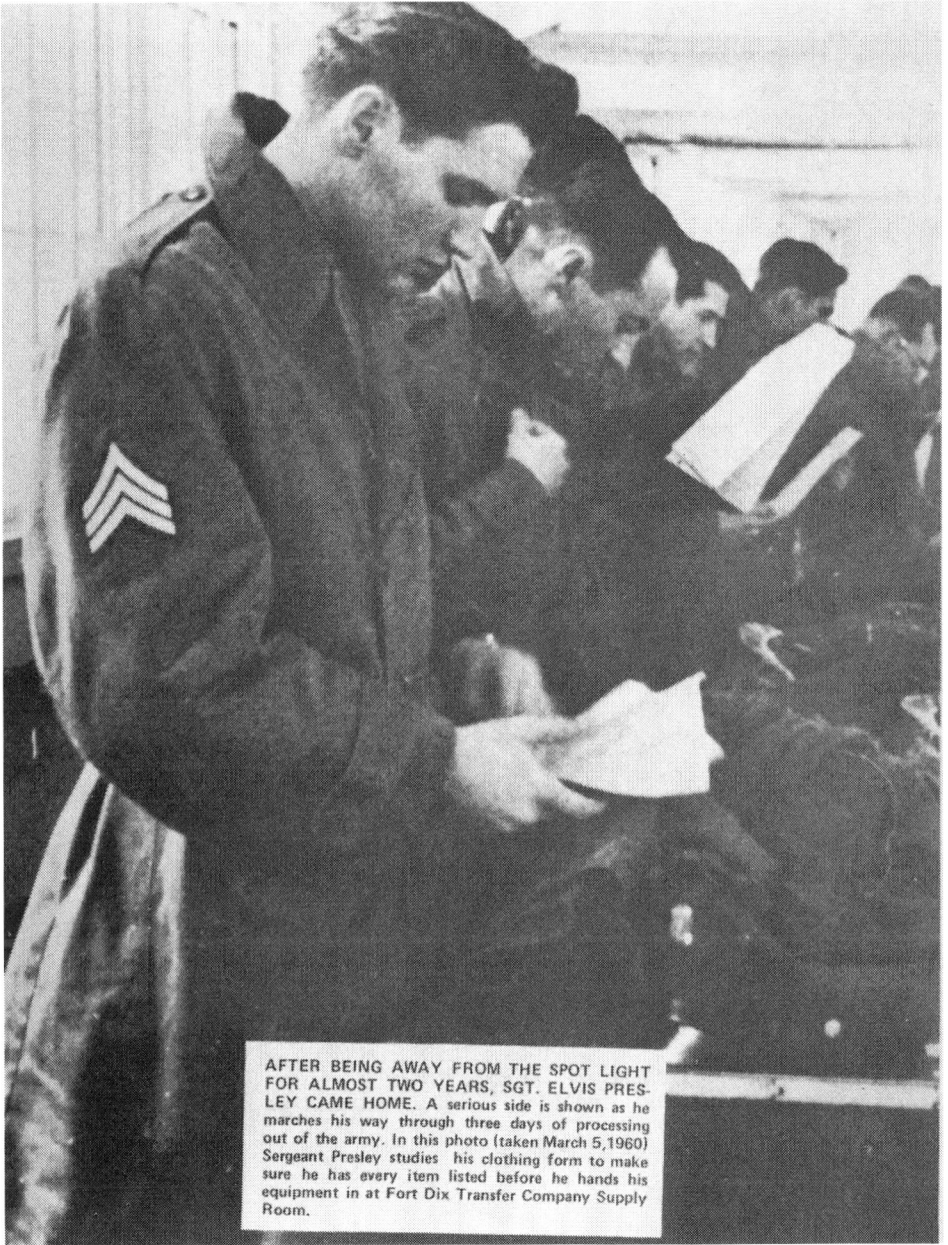

AFTER BEING AWAY FROM THE SPOT LIGHT FOR ALMOST TWO YEARS, SGT. ELVIS PRESLEY CAME HOME. A serious side is shown as he marches his way through three days of processing out of the army. In this photo (taken March 5, 1960) Sergeant Presley studies his clothing form to make sure he has every item listed before he hands his equipment in at Fort Dix Transfer Company Supply Room.

Elvis, Rex, and others on discharge orders turn in their army gear. (courtesy of U.S. Army)

Close-up of Rex during Life *magazine interview* (courtesy of *Life* magazine, March 1960)

Life *magazine photo of Rex taken during an interview during discharge processing at Fort Dix.* (courtesy of *Life* magazine, March 1960)

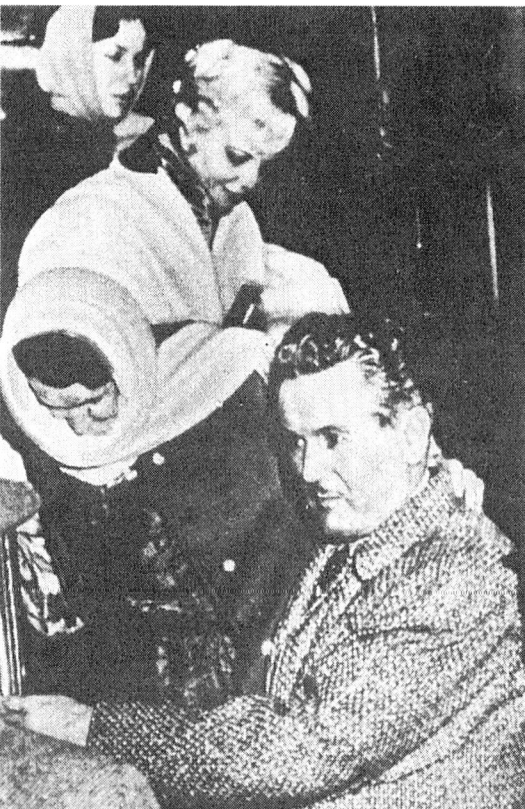

Elisabeth, Dee, Grandma, and Vernon arrive in Memphis by train.

Elvis' last photo to Elisabeth sent during Christmas 1960 from Colonel Parker's office

Rex places the wedding ring on Elisabeth's finger.

Elisabeth and Rex stand at the altar.

Rex's parents with Rex and Elisabeth on their wedding day

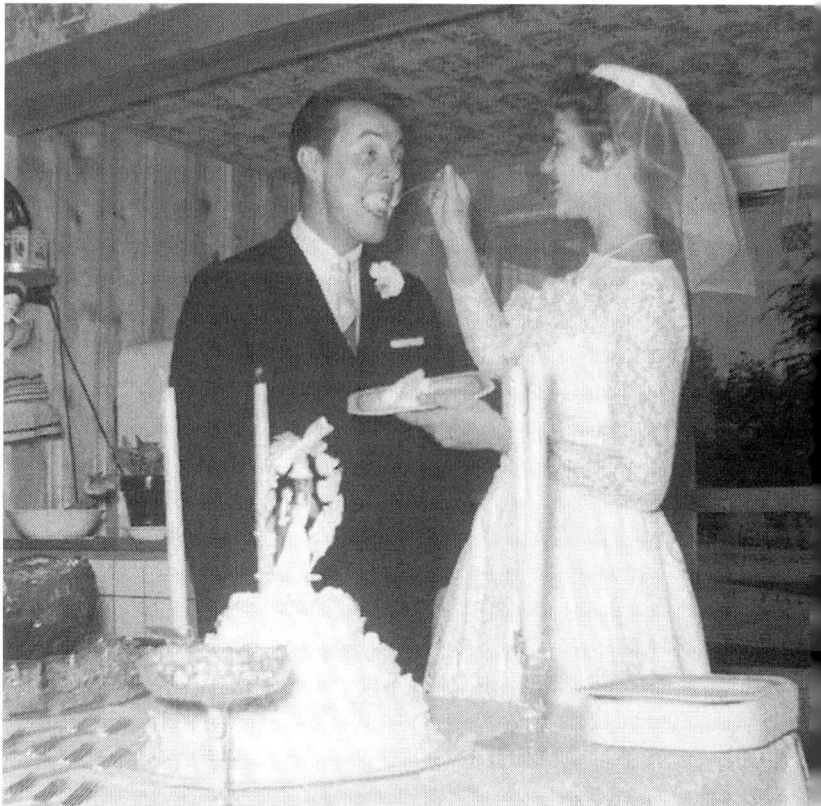

Elisabeth feeds wedding cake to Rex.

This photo of Elisabeth was used in a Dresden newspaper to announce her engagement and marriage to Rex.

Elisabeth at home in 1962

asked Elvis how he spent Christmas, about his projects coming up after his discharge, and wished him a happy birthday. Elvis told Clark that his first post-Army movie was going to be called *G.I. Blues*, and that he was already scheduled to make a television appearance singing a duet with Frank Sinatra.

Elvis threw himself a huge birthday party bash at the local recreation center. At least a couple of hundred people attended the party. A high percentage of those guests just happened to be female.

Most of the guys that were there were friends or acquaintances of Elvis', mostly GI's. Some of them brought girlfriends, but most of the girls there were free for the choosing, based on who could do the best selling job.

Priscilla was there for Elvis, which left Elisabeth free to dance with other guys. This became a problem in itself for the birthday boy and me.

Elvis and I were playing pool, taking on anybody that cared to challenge us. I was practically raised on a pool table, and while I was no Minnesota Fats, I more than knew my way around the 8-ball. Elvis wasn't too shabby, either, and there was nobody else there who could match us. When Elvis wasn't shooting, he had one arm around Priscilla. I kept both arms to myself, but at least one of my eyes followed Elisabeth around the room, and it seemed to me that she had a lot of dance partners. Since Elvis hadn't given her specific instructions on how to act, she did as she wanted and danced with anyone who asked her. It could be that she was defiantly showing Elvis that she could do whatever she pleased, and that there was nothing he could do about it because there were too many people around. Besides, how could he explain to Priscilla that Elisabeth was his girl, too?

After finishing a dance with Elisabeth, a GI I didn't know

walked her back by the pool table. He joined a friend, and the two were standing fairly close to where I was. I overheard Fred Astaire say something that made me nauseated.

"I think it's love at first sight," he boasted to a friend.

Of course he hadn't the slightest clue who I was and how I felt about Elisabeth, nor that she was Elvis' special girl. He was typical of the guys I had to fight off during my courtship with Elisabeth — 6-foot-2, dark and handsome, great dancer, and impeccable manners. He looked like the perfect catch for anybody, and in my galloping paranoia I had no trouble seeing Elisabeth fall for him. It was the curse of dating a beautiful woman.

After getting another earful of what this guy wanted to do with Elisabeth, I decided it was time to act. I was really in no position to tell this fellow that Elisabeth was off limits, but I knew somebody who was, and who would do it in no uncertain terms.

I told Elvis that a guy was trying to make out with Elisabeth. Then I pointed the wannabe Lothario out to him. Elvis instantly left Priscilla's side and marched right over to the guy to confront him. "Excuse me, but you're messin' with my girl, and no one gets away with that," Elvis told him. "You are no longer welcome here. I'm going to have to ask you to leave now or I'll have you thrown out."

This poor sucker was in a state of shock. He tried to explain that he didn't know Elisabeth was involved with Elvis. "Elvis, I'm sorry if there's some sort of misunderstanding," the guy said. "I didn't realize she was with you." Elvis just stood there glaring at him, and the poor guy stammered out another apology, and then slinked out of the door like a bastard at a family reunion.

Needless to say, I was beaming with pure delight. Siccing the ol' Hound Dog on Elisabeth's suitor was a stroke of genius, if I do say so myself. He could have been some real competition for me with Elisabeth. And I sure wasn't in the market for any more of that. Elvis was already more than I could handle.

CHAPTER SEVENTEEN

Walking Papers

Rex

Elvis took Lamar Fike, Cliff Gleaves, Joe Esposito, Jurgen Seydel, and Currie Grant back to Paris shortly after his birthday. Cliff had heard about our earlier adventures there and he was dying to go on another Paris road trip. Esposito was an Army company clerk from Chicago and a pal of Lamar's. Lamar persuaded Elvis to bring him along, too. I believe the main reason Elvis took Currie was as a reward for bringing Priscilla into his life.

While in Paris, Elvis planned to attend karate classes Seydel had arranged for him. Elvis was excited about taking more advanced instruction from Tetsuji Murakami, a world-famous Japanese karate instructor who specialized in the Shotokan technique. His plan was to train hard at the karate studio during the day, and then play even harder at his favorite clubs at night.

Elvis was kind enough to ask me to go along, but I had my own plans. I used the excuse that I was on duty every day that week and had no more leave due me. The real reason for staying behind, of course, was to spend more time with Elisabeth. With Elvis away, there would be no reason for the cloak-and-dagger stuff. We even ventured out in the open — at least to places we weren't likely to run into Vernon. It was the first time we dated outside of Rod and Vee's house. It was liberating and wonderful, and we really grew closer. Every second together was a godsend.

On January 24, 1960, our entire outfit was scheduled to join other Army outfits in Germany on maneuvers. It was the most intense and crucial winter training exercise we embarked on since coming to Germany. The Army appropriately named this 14-day event "Operation Snowshield."

The field trip was designed to test our combat readiness as well as to train us in extreme cold conditions. At that time, of course Russia was our Cold War enemy and the U.S. wanted us to be fully prepared. The Russians were already conditioned to the freezing temperatures, which helped them against the Germans in World War II. But frankly I was less concerned about the Russians and more preoccupied with my love life.

Elvis was busy with Priscilla, so Elisabeth and I met the night before we left for maneuvers at our usual place — the Harris' home. What a bittersweet night that was. We were elated to be in each other's company and savored every moment. But we faced a two-week separation, and my impending absence was already making our hearts grow fonder. As we embraced, I knew that Elisabeth was the only woman for me.

"I will miss you so much, dear. I promise to write you faithfully every single day," were her last words to me. We sealed the deal with a long kiss. I already couldn't wait for mail call.

"Operation Snowshield" took us into the middle of the Black Forest in southwest Germany. The Swiss border is along the southern end of the Black Forest, the French border runs along the southwest end, and the Bavarian, Swiss, and French Alps aren't far away. Under different circumstances, this would have been a beautiful, idyllic place. But it turned out to be where I spent the most miserable 14 days of my life.

I shiver thinking about it even today. We loaded up all the tanks and other track vehicles on flat cars and sent them on their way by train. All the soldiers traveled to the Black Forest in a convoy of 6 x 6 Army trucks. Once we arrived, we unloaded the tanks and other vehicles and drove them to the forest training areas while we tried with very limited success to keep from freezing to death. If stopping old Kruschev depended on us sitting there with German snow snakes up the rear, I wasn't sure I was up for the job.

It sure didn't help when we discovered the heaters in our tanks didn't work. The days were spent keeping ourselves and our equipment camouflaged so we couldn't be spotted by the "enemy" — U.S. soldiers dressed in foreign military garb. There was about two feet of snow on the ground and we all were cold enough to have "Mrs. Paul's" stamped on our foreheads. We were on what the Army called "blackout maneuvers," traveling only by night without lights. Using night-vision equipment, we could see just like in daytime. Our main 90-mm gun was equipped with a night-finder scope so the gunner could fire on targets at night. The M-48 tank had a lot of advanced technology that was exclusive to the military.

I saw Elvis only a few times in passing, and then just long enough for us to agree that this was the worst experience of our entire time in the Army. He was stationed at a benchmark or focal point, directing our tanks and support vehicles into an area in the Black Forest where we would bivouac for a day or so.

The whole battalion bivouacked in the same area, but Headquarters Company had its own separate area outside of the perimeter to act as forward guard to warn the line companies. All tank battalions had a headquarters company, which included the scout platoon to which Elvis was assigned, and four line companies comprised of A, B, C, and D Company, which did the actual fighting in case of war. The headquarters company also included other support platoons such as maintenance and mess service to keep the troops and equipment adequately running while on the move.

The V-12 Chrysler engines which powered our tanks had to be turned off immediately whenever we stopped. The big V-12 normally offered a good place to get warm if you could stand by the exhaust when it was running. Sometimes we would stay in one place for a couple of days and pitch our shelter halves in the snow. But sleep was impossible in the severe freezing weather. For most of the guys, that is.

I was already accustomed to going days without sleep thanks to the amphetamines. Elvis had sworn me to secrecy about the pills, so I never told anybody what I was taking. It was also dawning on me that the uppers were a crutch I was depending on more and more, so I wasn't about to start advertising it. My seemingly boundless energy was remarked on by more than one bleary-eyed GI.

Those little magic pills were sure powerless against the cold, though. A lot of guys got frostbite, mostly from not changing their socks often enough, or being otherwise lazy in their grooming procedures. Our instructors specifically gave us instructions on how to avoid frostbite: change our socks daily, and every time our feet got wet. If there was one good thing that came out of it for the frostbitten soldiers, it was that they got to go back to the Kaserne, albeit via the infirmary.

I was out in the cold in more ways than one. We had reached the halfway point of our maneuvers and I still hadn't heard word one from Elisabeth. Had I hallucinated her promise to write every day? With every day that passed without a letter, I became more depressed and disheartened.

Finally a letter arrived — the only one I would receive from Elisabeth during the entire two weeks. But instead of the juicy love letter I was expecting, her message was almost as formal as those long-ago greetings from President Eisenhower. Much more vague, too. At least Ike told me he wanted me. But Elisabeth wrote about the weather and mentioned a few visitors that dropped by the house. She mentioned that her and Grandma took a train to Grafenwohr and visited with her family for two days.

Whoopee!

I wanted steamy declarations of undying love and longing. Instead I got "Travels with Grandma." In my disappointment and anger I ripped the letter into tiny shreds so I wouldn't feel even worse by reading such tripe again.

Later, with my brain half-thawed out, I realized the emotional conflict building anew in Elisabeth. On one hand there was ol' Rex, just an everyday ordinary guy who loved her. On the other hand, the great Elvis Presley wanted her to go back to Memphis with him after the Army. He wanted her to live in the Graceland mansion and be his permanent private secretary. There had even been a promise from Elvis that she would go to Hollywood with him when he made movies. What girl wouldn't be tempted by such an exciting proposition? The odds against me were stacking up higher all the time.

"Operation Snowshield" finally ended, and by the time we returned to the Friedberg Kaserne my temperature had done a one-eighty. I was boiling mad. In fact, I had made up my mind to break it off with Elisabeth and forget about her altogether. She was the King's queen, and dethroning her would take a better man than me. I was so set on this course that I made no attempt to communicate with her for two weeks. She telephoned me every day at the Kaserne, but I never returned her calls.

I did visit the house in Bad Nauheim in that time, but I went out of my way to ignore Elisabeth. I had been hurt by her neglect on maneuvers, and now she was getting a taste of her own medicine. But a week later Elisabeth finally got a chance to speak to me — and I made sure she regretted it. Charge of Quarters (CQ) is a night duty all non-commissioned officers must pull, usually only one night every two weeks. Elisabeth got in touch with the company clerk I was scheduled to relieve when his regular duty was finished for the day. She begged him to reach me. He told her I would be pulling CQ that night, and was required to answer the phone on duty, so she could call me then. The clerk was a friend of mine, and he told me about Elisabeth's entreaty. So I had plenty of time to prepare myself for her call, and when the phone rang shortly after 10 p.m., I knew it was her. I answered on the first ring. Caught off guard, Elisabeth sounded surprised to finally reach me.

"Rex, is that you? Thank goodness I finally got through to you," she said. "Darling, I have been trying everyday to get in touch with you. I know you must be upset with me because I didn't write like I promised." I cut her right off and really let her have it. Both barrels were emptied as I called the girl I loved every dirty, nasty, rotten name in the book. I called her things I would be ashamed to repeat today. But all that pent-up frustration and heartache could not be denied, and the invective rolled on. When

I had finally run through my mental thesaurus of filthy words, I let her have it with Big Bertha. "I never want to see you again as long as I live!" I screamed into the phone.

"Rex! Rex, please don't hang up!" Elisabeth begged me through her tears. But I did. When Elisabeth called back several times, I hung up on her again and again. She wasn't the only one crying. Finally, when the telephone stopped ringing, I rushed into the restroom to wash away my tears. Good thing it was after curfew, so nobody was around to witness this horrible scene.

Then a strange thing occurred. It penetrated my thick Southern skull that I actually stood a chance with Elisabeth. If she still wanted things to work out for us even after my telephone tantrum, there must be hope after all. But did she want me as much as she wanted her life with Elvis? She had to know in no uncertain terms that she could not have us both.

If she really and truly loved me, she would want me even more after I cut her off so brutally, right? This was, after all, Colonel Parker's whole approach in selling Elvis to the public. Elvis told me many times how the Colonel would say, "Human nature says that people want what they cannot have." Now I was betting a lifetime of happiness on this theory.

It was now only a week or so before we would all be leaving for the States. Most were counting down the days, checking off each one on the calendar. We "short timers," as we were known, had to take inventory of the Army gear and equipment that we had been issued 17 months earlier. For Elvis, that meant turning in his jeep.

My responsibility was the tank and everything that went with it. I had maintained it meticulously since I was liable for anything missing or damaged. I didn't see much of Elvis while we were occupied with inventory and sign-offs. What little spare time he had was saved for Priscilla. I didn't miss him, though — my mind was still preoccupied with the love of my life, and my strategy to win her once and for all.

Elisabeth called John La Fatta daily to try to get through to me. Also, she had been sending notes through Vee. Elisabeth desperately wanted to see me one last time before we left for the States.

I finally agreed to meet her about the time I figured she might be thinking about giving up on me. Naturally, the meeting took place at Rod and Vee's house. I brought my good buddy John from the Kaserne with me, not only so I wouldn't have to be alone with her but because John was sort of my "Dear Abby," advising me on strategy. He was a stout shoulder for me to lean on, and was always there for me. When the time came that night, I was thoroughly prepped.

"Elisabeth, we need to wait until both of us return to the States before we can make any final decisions," I firmly told her. The idea was to hold out the absolute minimum of hope without saying anything concrete. The way I pulled it off, it should have been me heading into the starring role in *G.I. Blues* because what I really wanted to do was clutch Elisabeth in my arms and tell her how much I loved her.

I barely made it out of the house without breaking down. After I got in the taxi, I lost it completely. Heading back to the Kaserne I was overcome with grief, and ashamed of the way I pretended that Elisabeth's feelings were of little concern to me.

On March 1, 1960, the Army hosted its final press conference for Sergeant Presley. At 9 a.m., Elvis sat behind a table holding several microphones in the jam-packed Service Club at Ray Barracks.

A reporter questioned Elvis about his plans after the Army. "Well, the first thing I plan to do, naturally, is to go home. And then after that, I have a television show with Frank Sinatra, sometime in the later part of March. And then I start work on the picture *G.I. Blues* for Paramount. . . . Mr. Wallis. And then after that I have two pictures with 20th Century-Fox. And after that, heaven knows. . . . I don't," he answered with a laugh.

Another reporter asked Elvis if his military experience had been beneficial. "It's been a big help in both my career and my personal life, because I learned a lot, I made a lot of friends that I never would have made otherwise, and I've had a lot of good experiences . . . and some bad ones, naturally. It's good to rough it, to put yourself to a test, to see if you can take it, to see if you can stand it," he concluded with genuine sincerity.

What about me? Same question, Sgt. Mansfield. Well, I went along with Elvis. The Army taught me how to become my own man through discipline. I learned to take orders, and I learned how to give orders. I learned teamwork, and I learned how to recognize people's strengths and weaknesses. In short, I learned how to stand on my own two feet.

I wish that every young American male had to serve in our armed forces under the old draft system. I guarantee you, our country would be more patriotic and better off for it.

Serving with Elvis, of course, provided a bonus course in human relations. Being around him gave me an invaluable understanding about people and their motives. I have effectively used both my experience in the Army and time with Elvis to further my career in business as I climbed the ladder of success. I'm fairly certain I would not be where I am today without my Uncle Sam and my buddy Elvis.

On March 2nd, we were getting ready to fly out of Rhein-Main Air Base in Frankfurt. It was a cold and dreary day, similar to the one on which we had arrived. Our plane was scheduled to land at McGuire Air Force Base, right next door to Fort Dix, New Jersey. That's where, in a few more days, we would be officially discharged from the Army. Military service had benefited all of us in one way or another, but nobody was exactly sad to see it come to an end. We all felt relieved to be leaving Ray Barracks behind.

Vernon, Grandma, Lamar, and Elisabeth dropped by the Kaserne to say goodbye. I tried to act cool and unaffected, but in fact I was really glad to see Elisabeth on my last day in Germany. I shook Vernon's hand and gave Grandma a quick hug goodbye. I was concerned because Grandma did not look healthy and should not have been out in the cold weather. Knowing that I would be seeing Lamar a few days later, I joked around with him.

"Lamar, I'll see you back in the world, man," I said. The U.S. was commonly referred to by Americans on duty in Germany as "back in the world." It's what we knew best.

The glad-handing farewells over with, it was time to say goodbye to the beautiful woman I loved. But Elisabeth and I could only exchange glances. There was too much we had to leave unsaid, and it would be dangerous for me to even try a simple goodbye. For a brief moment I actually thought about declaring my undying love for her right then and there. I imagined how it would feel to sweep her off her feet and kiss her right in front of everyone — especially Elvis. But I held myself in check.

"Rex, save me a spot on the plane next to you," Elvis said. He planned on taking a taxi with Priscilla to the airport. I was going on the bus with the other GI's.

Without further acknowledging Elisabeth, I turned my back, looked down, and walked toward the bus. The charade was still on for Elvis, and Elisabeth still hadn't decided who she was going to end up with. I hoped I hadn't just made up her mind for her.

CHAPTER EIGHTEEN

Goodbye Germany, Hello Graceland

Elisabeth

During Elvis' last few weeks in Germany, Priscilla visited him more than ever.

I noticed Elvis treated her differently from all the other girls that he had been dating. For example, when Priscilla was in the room, his entire attention was focused on her. I knew he felt strongly about Priscilla by the way he looked at her, sat next to her, whispered in her ear. Other girls were just part of the scenery around him. Still, Elvis continued seeing other women after he met Priscilla. There might have been a few less women, but it was only because he had less time. He was definitely not what you'd call monogamous.

I had always believed Elvis was in love with Anita Wood. She had faithfully written him and eagerly awaited his return home. Elvis had been seeing Anita for two and a half years, and everyone thought they would end up getting married. Especially Anita.

I was surprised Anita never visited Elvis in Germany, but Vernon explained why it wasn't permitted. When Elvis was sent to Germany, Colonel Parker gave Elvis strict orders that Anita was not permitted to visit him until he returned home to Memphis. The Colonel wanted all the starry-eyed teenage girls to have the illusion that Elvis was still single and available. I found this out on one of my shopping trips with Vernon. I felt much more comfortable pumping Vernon for information than Elvis.

At that time in Elvis' life, he had so much respect for the Colonel that he obeyed his orders without question and never doubted his judgment. The direct result of such blind faith was increased revenue in record sales and merchandise. It also sealed Anita's fate forever, and allowed Priscilla to enter the picture.

Often I wanted to ask Elvis if he had fallen in love with Priscilla, but I knew better than to try. In fact, part of me would have been scared to hear his answer. My emotions were playing tug-of-war between Rex and Elvis. I was struggling to cope with my feelings, and became mentally exhausted. This made it difficult for me to write to Rex while he was away on maneuvers, as I had promised him I would.

I managed to write him one letter in which I discussed the weather, Grandma, and the gang. Nothing of interest to him. It certainly wasn't the passionate love letter he expected.

I didn't want to choose between Rex and Elvis. When I was alone with Rex, it was really special. I felt like I could spend the rest of my life with him. Rex was everything I wanted in a man. He was handsome, sweet, and affectionate. With Elvis, there was this rush of excitement that was hard to explain. Even with Priscilla and all the other females that hung around him, millions of girls would have killed to be in my shoes.

Right before Elvis left on his final maneuvers, he asked me to continue my duties as his private secretary in the States. This meant that I would live at Graceland, where I knew things would be much different. There would be movie stars coming around, big cars, maids, fancy furnishings and more. Any girl would be a fool to turn all that down. Besides, I loved my job. I was more confused than ever.

When Elvis and Rex both left for the field maneuvers, I had time to myself to do some thinking. I decided this would be a great opportunity to sort out my feelings. The office work went on as usual, but I spent more time talking with Grandma and Lamar. Whenever I confided in Grandma, she steered me in the direction of Rex. She would tell me how she adored him and what a good guy he was. She had a hunch Elvis would marry Anita Wood once he got back to Memphis. I had promised to write Rex everyday while he was away, but I didn't follow through. I was trying so hard to clear my head and straighten out my emotions. The two weeks flew by and I still hadn't come to any conclusions when the boys returned. I missed both Rex and Elvis, and was really looking forward to having both of them home.

I was disappointed that Rex did not come by the house. He must have told Elvis he was on duty, because Elvis didn't think it unusual. My intuition told me something was wrong between Rex and me. When Rex finally did come to the house, he completely ignored me. His behavior only confirmed my feelings. I was worried about losing Rex and made up my mind to track him down somehow.

Finally one evening I managed to reach him by phone. Unfortunately, a side of him came out that I never knew existed. I was called horrible names and accused of everything under the sun. It was totally out of character for Rex. To add insult to injury, he hung up on me several times.

After this, I thought he never wanted to see me again and our relationship was over. I couldn't believe that this sweet, polite, gentle man was being so horrible.

Part of me was angry, thinking that no one should talk to me that way and get away with it. I also understood that what I did to him was wrong and he was truly hurt. I never blamed Rex for being mad when he returned home from the field, because I had broken my promise to him.

In the past, Rex was always easy to get along with and very polite to everyone. I assumed he would be the type of husband that a woman could wrap around her little finger. I thought the phone conversation was bad, but the worst was yet to come.

Rex agreed to meet at our mutual friends' house for dinner. I was surprised to see that Rex brought his friend, John La Fatta. Of course, John knew our secret. All through dinner, Rex avoided eye contact with me and I sensed his anger. After dinner, Rex decided to let me have it, with John's help. He didn't hold back either. Everything that bothered him came out in harsh words. Accusations were hurled at me with no opportunity for me to defend myself. Rex let me know that our future would remain on hold until we returned to the States. Next thing I knew, Rex and John disappeared in a taxi.

I sat there with my head in my hands, tears streaming down my cheeks, trying to figure out what happened. I wondered if Rex would ever have anything to do with me again. Vee came to my side and I told her everything.

"You know Rex didn't mean what he said, honey. He is just hurt and upset, but you two will make up," Vee said, wiping the tears from my face. The next day I told Grandma what happened and she agreed with Vee.

"If it's meant to be, you two will be together in the end," Grandma said in a very loving tone. It was nice to have her shoulder to cry on since I was away from my parents.

My stepfather had received orders for Fort Campbell, Kentucky, and they were leaving a few weeks before us. Elvis asked me to stay and help out until he was ready to leave Germany. Elvis wanted to pay my way to Memphis so I could travel with Vernon, Grandma, and Lamar.

A week before we left for Memphis, Grandma got sick and had to stay in bed. It was fortunate that Elvis had asked me to stay, because I was able to really pitch in and help that last week. During the entire stay in Germany, Grandma was never sick, so the timing was rotten.

Priscilla came as often as possible in the final days to spend time with Elvis. Usually Vernon and Lamar drove to Wiesbaden to bring her to the house, and returned her home. Since Priscilla was in school, she was not allowed to stay out late. She told me that her parents did not appreciate the times she got back later than they expected. Priscilla said she would have to think up lies to tell her parents to explain why she was late. Usually she blamed the heavy fog for missing her curfew.

By this time, I was getting used to her coming around, and it was clear that Elvis was completely taken with her. I just wasn't ready to let go of him.

The final week before we were to leave Germany was nerve-racking. I had to pack all of Grandma's belongings since she was ill. I really loved her and was genuinely concerned. In a sense, we had adopted each other. We were all concerned about her making the long trip ahead. I also had to pack all of Elvis' things, and he had accumulated quite a lot during his 17 months in Germany. It was rather hectic. Not knowing where I stood with Rex or Elvis didn't make it much easier. I was on pins and needles.

The day before our departure, Frau Pieper and her lawyer asked to speak to Elvis and his dad. I was included in the meeting, acting as the translator. I was shocked that she had a lawyer, and I knew something was up. I smelled a rat — a fuss-budgety old German one.

My suspicions were correct. Frau Pieper didn't want Elvis to get away without leaving a bundle of money behind. She wanted money for every scratch put on the furniture, even though Elvis already paid a large sum of money for renting the furnished house. The Presley men told me to explain to the plaintiffs that they paid more than enough rent to cover any small damages to the furniture. Frau Pieper and her lawyer threatened to bring a lawsuit, as well as to bring reporters in to view the house. Elvis did not want any negative publicity, so he agreed to pay a large sum of money to the scam artists.

This was another classic example of how Elvis was taken advantage of because of his fame and fortune. It was a crash course in human behavior for me, being around Elvis and learning how ugly and greedy some people could be. I was just thankful we wouldn't have to associate with Frau Pieper any longer, and thought about taking a few whacks at her crummy furniture myself on the way out, since the damage was already paid for.

Elvis and Rex were leaving on the same day, but not with us. The Army was flying Elvis and Rex, along with a planeload of other soldiers who were on their way to be discharged or transferred to new duty back in the States. After their discharge at Fort Dix, they would take a train to Memphis. The rest of us would be flying to New York via commercial airlines, and then into Memphis.

On March 2, 1960, Lamar, Grandma, and I drove to the Kaserne to bid farewell to Elvis. But it was Rex I was secretly hoping to see.

Priscilla and Rex were there, along with many photographers. I got my wish to see Rex, but because of Elvis' strict edict, I could not speak directly to him. While we didn't have the opportunity to talk, our eyes locked a few times. I feared I was losing both men, and it was an emotionally charged day for me.

At a moment when Priscilla was out of earshot, Elvis had some special instructions for me. "Darlin', I'm counting on you to take extra special care of Grandma," he whispered quietly. He also assured me that we would see each other in about a week.

We took a taxi to Frankfurt Airport after Elvis and Rex boarded their plane. Thankfully, we made our plane to New York just in time to board. Once in our seats, Grandma slept through most of the flight as she was still not healthy. I almost envied her. I couldn't sleep since I was a bundle of nerves, thinking about what the future would hold for me.

Our luggage was checked, and we cleared customs without any complications. I was lucky because the day before we left Germany, Elvis handed me an enormous bottle of his special pills to take to Graceland.

"Here, Foghorn, take this back to Memphis in your suitcase and keep them safe for me until I get there," Elvis said, winking. I knew these pills were the ones he and the other guys took every day, but I didn't realize at the time the trouble that I could get into for smuggling prescription drugs into America without a prescription. The amount of amphetamines in Elvis' bottle could have filled up a half-gallon glass jar. Since I didn't have a prescription, there could have been serious repercussions had I been checked. I was totally naive on this matter. Colonel Tom Parker met us at the airport in New York and took us to a hotel to spend the night. He called in a doctor for Grandma, and she was diagnosed with a severe case of the flu.

After hearing so much about the Colonel, it was nice to finally meet him. I could readily see that he was a very calculating man, and everything he did seemed to work out as smooth as silk. He seemed preoccupied, but worked diligently to get us squared away for our train trip to Memphis. Elvis would be following us shortly, coming in that same day to Fort Dix a few hours later.

The next morning, Vernon, Grandma, and I boarded the train to Memphis, Tennessee. I assumed we would take a plane to Memphis, but Vernon preferred the train. Soon I learned the reason for his choice of transportation. Dee had left Germany and joined her sister in Norfolk, Virginia. The plan was for Dee to drive from Richmond to Norfolk, Virginia, to meet our train. From there, she would head into Memphis with us.

When we arrived at the main train station in Memphis, there was a mass of reporters snapping pictures. I accidentally called Dee's name within earshot of the press, which angered Vernon. He did not want the reporters to know her identity; he warned me not to "let the cat out of the bag."

The following day the Memphis papers published pictures of our arrival. Everybody was wondering about the identity of the mystery woman who got off the train with Vernon. She was rushed into hiding and did not go directly with the rest of us to the Graceland Mansion. It's possible that Dee had not gotten her final divorce decree at the time, which would explain the secrecy involved; but that's only my guess.

Dee was placed in a taxi by Vernon and met up with us later

at Graceland. Vernon, Grandma, and I took a separate taxi. I could hardly wait to see Graceland as we passed through the wrought-iron gates.

Stepping out of the car, I tuned out all the people and noise surrounding me. I pretended as if I were all alone so I could really concentrate. This was my first time at Graceland, and I wanted it to be special. I wanted to savor this moment. I slowly looked up at the mansion, etching every detail in my mind.

Breathtaking is the only way I could express my first vision of Graceland. It was even bigger and better than I had seen in movie magazines. The four huge white columns holding up the front pediment were spectacular against the backdrop of the beautiful Tennessee gray stone walls. It looked to me like one of the mansions out of *Gone with the Wind*.

If I thought the outside was magnificent, I was completely awe-struck when I stepped inside and saw the winding stairway graced with white handrails and red carpet. I took my time and spent hours walking from room to room, and found Graceland to be tastefully and elegantly decorated. After all, if this was to be my new home, I should get to know the place.

The resident cook had been in the Presley mansion for many years, and gave Vernon and Grandma a warm welcome. She was extremely busy since she also doubled as a maid.

In Germany, Grandma ruled the kitchen like a fiefdom. But once she came back home to Graceland, she relinquished all of her cooking duties and did whatever pleased her. She had performed admirably in Germany and now was going to take a much-needed rest. I never saw Grandma cook another meal again.

Vernon showed me the room I would be staying in, which was next to Grandma's. I felt like a princess just discovering her magical castle. When Vernon showed me his room, I noticed Mrs. Presley's clothes and personal items were still intact. This could also be why Dee Stanley stayed behind.

For the next few days, I did not have to work on any fan mail. My office had not been sorted out yet, and all of us were still waiting for Elvis to arrive from New Jersey. I kept myself occupied by looking around the house and visiting with Grandma, who was on the mend.

There were several garages full of Cadillacs, Lincoln limousines, and motorcycles. There was a large house in behind the mansion where Elvis' uncle lived. He guarded the front gate. Rex had already described to me the inside of the house, but even after seeing it for myself, I had a hard time processing the grandeur.

Janie Wilbanks, who resided in Memphis at the time, came over for a visit. Grandma and I were delighted to see her and the three of us acted like schoolgirls, chatting away and catching up.

When Grandma excused herself, I told Janie all about the details of my secret relationship with Rex and how I was agonizing with indecision when it came to him and Elvis. She was very sympathetic and encouraged me to think seriously about choosing a life with Rex.

"Honey, you and I both know how Elvis is," Janie said. "He's not going to settle down with any one girl when he doesn't have to. Look at how he's been stringing along poor Anita Wood. It's been more than two years."

Anita also came to the house and visited with Grandma. I found her to be as nice as she was attractive. I viewed Anita as somewhat of a celebrity because she co-hosted a local television show, and looked as glamorous as any Hollywood movie star. I had read about her for years in entertainment magazines and heard her voice many times on the Andy Williams record, "Hawaiian Wedding Song," which Elvis played over and over in Germany. He told me that while her name was not on the record itself, she sang the words, "I do, love you, with all my heart." It was a sly way of telling Elvis how she felt about him.

Elvis and Rex would be arriving any minute and I was as torn as ever between them. For the life of me, I just could not come to a final decision. Would Graceland become my permanent home, or would Rex take me away?

It was March 7, 1960, when Elvis arrived at Graceland with Colonel Parker, Tom Diskin (the Colonel's assistant), Rex Mansfield, Lamar Fike, and Ken Moore (a professional wrestler from Fort Worth). Anita Wood, his old sweetheart, was nervously pacing up and down the floor of the big kitchen. Unless Anita was a monk or had been living under a rock, she must have read about Priscilla while Elvis was in Germany.

The entrance at the back of the house was through the kitchen and this was the way Elvis always came in. Some of the relatives, as well as old friends, were waiting to greet him. I had heard so much about all these people I felt comfortable with them, like I was a part of the group. Finally Elvis arrived, and the room filled up with hugs and kisses.

A bit later, when Elvis went to the gates to sign autographs, Rex managed to whisper a few words to me in private.

"If you ever want to see me again, you're going to be the one who makes the call," Rex said. "I think I've laid all my cards on the table, and then some." Then he was gone. Elvis spent the rest of the evening having fun with all his friends. This gave me time to contemplate Rex's ultimatum.

The next evening Elvis brought out one of his sporty motorcycles to take us out for a spin. "Foghorn, I'm going to take you for a motorcycle ride," he said. There were still several fans waiting by the gate, but we sped right through. Cars began to chase us, but Elvis lost them. He drove through the streets of Memphis with no particular destination in mind. Elvis loved being behind a motorcycle, as it reminded him of his carefree days before going into the Army. I was flattered he asked me to go on this ride. There were plenty of other people, but he picked me. In the back of my mind I had worried that when Elvis was home, and surrounded by all his friends, I wouldn't be very important to him anymore. After all, in Bad Nauheim, we were a small group and things were different.

The next day there was an article in the Memphis paper reporting that Elvis was spotted on a motorcycle with an "unidentified girl." What a great feeling to know that unidentified girl just happened to be me!

My excitement was short-lived, because all of a sudden Elvis told me he was "lifting my restrictions." Now that we were in America, it would be acceptable for me to date again. I felt both relieved and at the same time hurt by this surprise turnabout. I never felt guilty about seeing Rex behind Elvis' back, since Elvis dated many other women. Now I could date Rex in the open.

I wondered why Elvis all of a sudden decided to change his long-standing policy regarding me and other men. Did he not care for me as much as before? Was it because of Anita? I should have been grateful to be off the hook, but I was depressed actually.

The following day, Elvis and his buddies left Graceland and went into the city for a couple of hours. Upon his return, Elvis took my hand and led me to the front of the house. In the driveway he pointed to the most brilliant yellow Lincoln Continental I have ever seen.

"Here darlin', it's all yours," Elvis said as he handed me the keys. I was overwhelmed with joy because Elvis actually hand-picked the car especially for me. It wasn't a brand new 1960 model, but to me it was the most beautiful car I had ever seen, and I was the proud owner.

I spent hours driving my car around and around the circular driveway in front of the mansion. I was like a kid on Christmas morning playing with a new toy. My very first car was a gift to me from Elvis Presley. I had received my driver's license at age 16 in Maryland. My license was expired because during the last three years in Germany I had not driven. I was not very confident behind the wheel, and explained to Elvis I needed to practice in order to get a new license.

Later that evening, Elvis drove me to a big parking lot in Memphis in a different car. We switched places and Elvis guided me while I drove. These latest developments had me really confused. After all, he could have sent Lamar to buy me the car and teach me how to drive. Instead, he personally took care of these things.

Talk about mixed messages! It took me a while, but I finally figured out that Elvis was trying to let me down as gently as possible. He was always perceptive concerning other people's feelings, and perhaps he knew how much it hurt me when he told me I was free to date other men. Things were suddenly becoming very clear in my mind. In staying with Elvis, I would only be his private secretary. I could leave with Rex and be his one and only. That was it — my mind was made up.

In a moment that seemed positively surreal, I telephoned Rex that evening at his home in Dresden. "You're the one I want to be with," I whispered into the phone. I explained that Elvis had released me to date others so, if he would come back to

Graceland, we could go out together and talk everything over. I also mentioned that I was calling from a phone line at Graceland and someone could be listening, so I couldn't say everything I felt in my heart. Rex sounded so happy, and assured me that he would come back to Graceland in the next few days.

"Don't you worry, honey, I promise everything will work out for us," he assured me. When I hung up the phone, I knew I made the right decision.

Before Rex made his way back to Memphis, Anita invited me to spend the night with her. It was obvious to Elvis that she wanted to pump me for information about what he did with his free time in Germany. I didn't ask Elvis for his permission — I straight out told him I was going.

"Foghorn, now you be careful what you say to Anita," Elvis warned. Then he softened his tone and added, "And what she don't know won't hurt her." He then winked at me with his sheepish grin. Part of me wanted to spill my guts to Anita because of how Elvis had hurt my feelings, yet at the same time, I felt like everyone else in his entourage, and wanted to protect Elvis.

Spending the night with some female companionship was a nice change of pace, and I also enjoyed the freedom of being away from Graceland. It was clearer than ever that I needed to leave for good with Rex. As for Anita, eventually she did get around to asking some hardball questions, but did it in a "soft-sell" manner.

"Elisabeth, you'll just have to tell me all about Elvis and any of the girls he had anything to do with for the past two years," Anita said. She wasn't a shy girl by any means.

I was very careful with my answers and didn't tell her anything that she hadn't already read in the fan magazines. When the moment of truth came, I protected both Elvis and Anita. She asked me about Margit Buergin, Janie Wilbanks, and Priscilla Beaulieu. "Oh, he didn't date anyone too seriously that I can recall," I said, not wanting to hurt her. "He doesn't tell me how he feels about other girls." Basically, I pleaded ignorance.

Anita was a sweet person, and I liked her very much. It would only wound her if she knew how Elvis behaved in Germany. In a way, I truly felt sorry for her. I knew she genuinely loved Elvis — maybe even more than I once did. That was the problem with Elvis and his women, he eventually hurt all of them with his promiscuous behavior.

Later that night, Anita took me to a nightclub. We were entertained by the music of a then unknown singer by the name of Charlie Rich, who later went on to achieve great success. I enjoyed her company, but we didn't have time to really bond. I turned to Janie when I needed help.

Janie knew exactly how Elvis operated — she was a casualty just like me. I trusted her completely and knew she would support me. She knew about my secret relationship with Rex. I told her that I made my decision and I wanted to be with Rex. "Elisabeth, you know I will help you any way I can," Janie said, instantly becoming my new best friend.

I was very nervous awaiting Rex's arrival and wondered how Elvis would react. I knew Rex was his own man and would stand up to Elvis if he had to.

Rex came the next day, and he and Elvis got reacquainted. Elvis enjoyed being with his old friends at Graceland and reminiscing with Rex about their Army days. There was some obvious male bonding taking place, and I felt like a square peg in a round hole.

After the opening pleasantries, Rex forged ahead with his mission. "Elvis, could I speak to you in private for a few minutes?" he asked. Elvis led Rex upstairs to his bedroom.

The moment of truth had arrived.

CHAPTER NINETEEN
Planes, Trains, and Automobiles

Rex

As soon as the rest of us GI's arrived at the airplane passenger loading zone in the Rhine-Main air base, we got off the bus. I made a point to be first off and first up the steps to the plane. I hustled to the rear of the plane and selected the last two rear seats for Elvis and me. We were flying in a U.S. Air Force Military Air Transport (MAT) plane. I believe these planes were privately owned and leased to the military with pilots and crew.

Elvis boarded from the rear to keep a low profile. Only a few people knew that he was going to be on the plane. At 5:25 p.m., we took off from Frankfurt and headed for McGuire Air Force Base, where we would be discharged in the same military complex at Fort Dix, New Jersey.

News that Elvis Presley was one of the passengers spread like wildfire. The stewardesses were overjoyed and excited. A lot of them joined a line of passengers, mostly female dependents of other GI's on the plane, for autographs. After about two hours of this, Elvis told me he was tired and wanted to get some sleep.

"Rexadus, it's time for me to get some shut-eye. How 'bout you act as my bodyguard and spokesman for awhile?" he said. There would be all kinds of press waiting at Fort Dix and Elvis needed to be as fresh as possible. After all, this would be his first time back in America in 17 months. I obliged Elvis by standing up in the aisle and acted as a human blockade between him and his fans. In addition, I played the role of publicist, fielding questions from the curious.

"Did Elvis sing any songs while he was in the Army?"

"What's it like being his close friend?"

"Have you ever been to Graceland before?"

"Were you friends with Elvis before going into the Army?"

"What's Elvis going to do now?"

I was relieved when the stewardess requested that every passenger return to his seat. I was worn out by this time and quickly fell asleep.

After a few hours, we stopped to refuel and stretch our legs. The plane trip went by quickly and we gained about six hours on the clock, which of course also meant we lost that much sleeping time. Our flight to McGuire AFB was uneventful until the plane came in for a landing. New Jersey in early March can be cold, with lots of snow and ice, and now the snow was falling so thick that we could not see the runway until just before the plane landed. The pilot came down off-center on the runway and had to quickly go hard left. The plane swerved and the left wing almost touched the runway. By the grace of God, our pilot managed to get things under control and bring us to a stop.

There was a big crowd waiting to welcome home America's favorite soldier. Cameras were flashing and TV camera crews rushed about. Colonel Parker was there along with his assistant,

Tom Diskin, and Lamar Fike. A big press conference was scheduled right away. We hit the bricks running. Where getting the King back in the public eye was concerned, there wasn't a second to lose.

This was my first actual face-to-face meeting with the Colonel. He was in charge of everything that happened with Elvis' career, and apparently that also went for Elvis' friends, because Parker told me to give an interview to *Life* magazine. Even before I was officially out of the Army, I was answering to a different colonel. "Rex, don't say anything negative about Elvis or the Army," he commanded.

I bent over backwards to follow orders, with the result that none of my bland quotes were ever published in *Life*.

I was invited on the train ride home to Memphis with the Colonel, Elvis, Tom, Lamar, and Ken Moore. After nearly 17 months away, it was great to be back in "the real world," although, come to think of it, being around Elvis Presley was about as unreal as it gets.

We were discharged from the Army on March 5, 1960, although our official date of release was down as March 23, 1960. I suppose early releases from the Army happen all the time, but it did occur to me that maybe the deft hand of Colonel Parker might be responsible for the early release.

We spent three days at Fort Dix mustering out. The constant commotion between Elvis and the press was even greater now than when he was inducted into the Army. The increased focus was understandable, because Elvis had been a model soldier and had gained more respect than ever. The Colonel had pulled it off. Having Elvis pull his military service just like any other GI was paying huge dividends — publicity-wise, if not financially.

We received our muster-out pay of $109.54. Immediately upon receipt of our final discharge papers, the Colonel quickly transported Elvis and me in a limousine from Fort Dix to our secret hideaway, a hotel in Trenton, New Jersey. We left undetected, which was the Colonel's specialty. It was a fairly invisible leave-taking, because Parker wanted us to get as much rest as possible for the carnival the Colonel had secretly arranged when we traveled to Memphis. We checked out of our hotel very late the next morning, and at roughly noon we boarded our private railroad lounge car.

Forget that Paris business — the most memorable 48 hours of my life were coming up all aboard the Elvis Express! Tom, Lamar, and Ken joined Elvis, the Colonel, and me in the lounge car. Elvis told me it belonged to the president of the railroad. I didn't doubt that — it was absolutely plush, with red carpet and all the bells and whistles.

Our first stop was Washington, D.C., where we changed trains and boarded a sleeper car that was at the very end of the train. In front of our car was another private lounge car that we also used on the trip to Memphis.

Our itinerary was supposed to be a secret from the press. But like a lot of Colonel Parker's "secrets," this one traveled faster than the speed of sound. Of course, the idea was to wring the maximum PR value out of Elvis' homecoming. One well-planted Parker "secret" was like the Bat Signal over Gotham City: it brought the troops running. Sure enough, every place we stopped en route to Memphis, there were between 500 and 1,000 fans waiting to catch a glimpse of the conquering hero.

It was also no accident that our sleeper car was the last one on the train. This way Elvis could stand out on the rear platform to greet his fans and sign autographs, just like a whistle-stop politician (only more popular). While screaming and crying, some of the young girls chased the train down the tracks as we pulled out. Elvis' return from the Army was a reminder to his fans of how much they had missed him. He was more popular than ever.

Just after midnight we made another "top secret" stop, this one in Roanoke, Virginia. Elvis was sound asleep and the Colonel didn't want to wake him as he wanted Elvis well-rested and ready for the arrival in Memphis the next day. But, as at all the previous stops, there were clamoring fans waiting there in spite of the late hour, hoping for at least a fleeting look at the returning Tennessee country boy who'd made good.

Colonel Parker asked me to stand out on the platform when the train started pulling away from the Roanoke station. I was still wearing my green uniform, and with the Army hat plopped on my head by Colonel Parker, I easily passed my last inspection. From a distance of 50 yards or so, who knew I wasn't the world's greatest rock 'n' roller? Not the hundreds of screaming fans at the Roanoke station. As we pulled away, I stepped out on the platform and began waving and blowing kisses to the adoring fans, and the place went nuts.

"King for a day," I chuckled to myself as we rolled away. But for a few brief moments, I felt the sensation that Elvis must have felt over and over when his fans saw him. It was great, sure, but with that going on around a person every time he appeared in public, any chance for a normal life was over. I both envied Elvis and felt sorry for him. How could a guy ever just get to be himself in such an atmosphere? Maybe that was an odd question from somebody who'd just become the only authorized Elvis impersonator on record.

At any rate, the next morning everyone was up early and antic-ipating our arrival in Memphis later in the day. I remember thinking that if this day turned out any more exciting than the one before, I didn't know if I could stand it.

Somewhere between Roanoke and Memphis I reached a final decision about whether I would go with Elvis, or leave him to be with Elisabeth. It would be impossible to do both. If he ever even allowed me to marry Elisabeth, how could I still travel with him, being around all those girls all the time, and still stay true to Elisabeth? It also occurred to me that if Elvis ever found out I had been seeing her secretly in Germany, he would not trust me any longer. And since so many other people around Elvis already knew about Elisabeth and me, sooner or later he would have to find out. Should I just come clean and tell him myself? Now I found myself in the same position as Elisabeth. I didn't want to give anything up.

To take my mind off the situation, I watched Elvis shooting dice for $100 a throw. He was well-aware that neither Lamar nor I could afford that kind of high rolling, so he handed us each a couple of $100 bills so we could play, too. I got lucky and within 30 minutes I was up $500. When we finished playing, I offered all my money to Elvis. He wouldn't accept it. Then I tried to at least give him back the $200 he had spotted me to get in the game, and he wouldn't take that, either. I think Elvis was impressed that I attempted to pay him back. But why wouldn't I? It was his money.

We were standing alone at one end of the private lounge car, and what happened next was a roll of the dice I never expected, with "Jackpot" written all over it. "Rexadus, there is a lot more money than this $500 waiting for you, if you will come to work for me and be my number-one aide," Elvis said. My starting salary would be $100 per week in cash, all taxes paid, he said. And that wasn't all.

"I'll furnish your clothes, you'll have a new car of your choice every year, and I'll pay for all of your personal and living expenses," Elvis continued. Then came the capper: "Rexadus, you'll live the same life as me," Elvis said. "You go where I go and do what I do."

As a veteran salesman myself, I knew a great sales pitch when I heard one, and this beat anything that ever came my way before. It was an offer only a fool would refuse — a fool in love. I guess there isn't a guy in the world besides me who would not have jumped at the bait right then. But Elvis had unknowingly put me in yet a deeper hole. I didn't know what to say. I just stood there, dumbfounded. Noting my condition, Elvis gently told me, "You don't have to give me an answer this minute — think it over, Rexadus."

Man, was I ever glad he said that. But even Elvis couldn't resist another slight turn of the screws.

"Think of all the good times we'll have," he said, resting his arm on my shoulder. When Elvis really wanted you on his stringer, he really knew how to set the hook. When I still stood there slack-jawed, Elvis suggested that I talk things over with Colonel Parker.

I was agreeable to that, but consulting the Colonel presented a different problem. I wasn't sure how much Parker knew about me, but what really concerned me was how much, if anything, he knew about me and Elisabeth. I shouldn't have even wondered, because if anything ever got by Tom Parker, it wasn't worth noticing to begin with. About 20 years later, I found out the Colonel had in fact known about Elisabeth's and my involvement. As soon as Lamar landed back in the States from Germany, the Colonel sat him right down for a debriefing that would've made the C.I.A. proud. Lamar said that Elvis would be interested in keeping me with him, but that I was in a spot because of my feelings for Elisabeth. Parker told Lamar that he would handle the situation without getting anybody hurt.

Elvis arranged for me to see the Colonel in private. Parker listened intently as I reviewed Elvis' startling job offer, his face impassive except for those shrewd eyes. I said that I genuinely liked Elvis and wanted only the best for him (Elisabeth excepted, though I kept that thought to myself). I also mentioned several other career opportunities open to me in the business world, and solicited the Colonel's honest advice on the matter.

Then came the second big sucker punch of my morning, in a clear and calm manner, the Colonel told me in so many words that he thought I was smart enough to make it on my own, and that I didn't need Elvis.

"Rex, you're not like most of the other guys that hang around Elvis," he said. "You've got a lot more on the ball. Now son, you don't have to listen to me. My advice is free and it doesn't cost anything, so it may not be worth nothin'. If you want to go with Elvis, by all means, do so," he said. Then he suggested that I go home for a few days to think things out, and then return to Graceland with my final answer.

The most important thing, Parker admonished, was that I say nothing to Elvis about his position on the matter. "If you tell Elvis that I told you not to take the job, I'll deny it," he said. Elisabeth never came up in the conversation. But as I learned later from Lamar, the Colonel knew about us and foresaw problems down the road.

Whatever his motivation, my session with Parker made up my mind. I was choosing love, because love is forever. I was an independent man and would make my own way in the world. There were plenty of guys standing in line to serve Elvis, but I was no longer one of them. I have never regretted that decision for one day, and I am grateful to the Colonel for his insight.

I choked up telling Elvis that I would not give him an answer until after I had been home for a few days. When I told him the Colonel had advised me to do so, Elvis assumed everything was going his way.

"Rexadus, I told you the Colonel would tell you to go with me," Elvis said with a smile. "I'm sure he did just that even though he advised you to wait a few days to make your final decision," Elvis said. I said nothing, and we went on to other things.

Would I have gone with Elvis if, as he thought, the Colonel had encouraged me to do so? Ultimately, I don't know the answer, but I can say for sure that my decision came easily after speaking with the Colonel.

It was an unforgettable scene when we stepped off the train at Memphis' Union Station. Throngs of screaming, hysterical girls welcomed home the city's favorite son. I took it all in stride — after all, nobody was screaming my name.

It was March 7, 1960, and in my pocket were discharge papers and my $500 craps game winnings. Behind me were almost two years as a U.S. Army tank commander and a close, close friendship with Elvis Presley. It was awfully good to be back in my home state. We were met by a couple of Elvis' old friends and ushered into two cars. It was a trick getting through the crowds, even with local police and the Highway Patrol running interference. Lamar, Tom, and I went in the car that served as a decoy. Needless to say, the only screams, when the girls followed us and discovered it was just me, were pure anguish.

More herds of people were gathered at the Graceland gate,

and Elvis came in through the back way. Later, however, he went down to the gate to sign autographs. Meanwhile, I called my brother Doyle and let him know I was ready to be picked up. I had already arranged for him to be in Memphis on the day we arrived. He was waiting for me at his brother-in-law's house, which was fairly close to Graceland.

By God's grace, I managed to sneak a private moment with Elisabeth. I found her at the bottom of the stairs in the foyer of the house. From where we stood we could see Elvis through the front windows, signing autographs. Since I knew our time together was limited, I did not mince words.

"If you ever want to see me again, call me at home in Dresden," I said firmly, slipping her my parents' phone number. "I will not call you," I emphasized. "You must call me."

Before she could even answer, we noticed Elvis was heading back to the house. Elisabeth disappeared immediately. We did not want Elvis to see us alone, especially on his home turf.

Elvis came to let me know my brother had arrived. I told him I would be back in a week to give him my final answer, although, in fact, I never intended to come back if Elisabeth did not call. Elvis walked me to the front door and patted me on my back.

"See you real soon, buddy," he said warmly.

I hadn't seen Doyle in a long time, and normally it would be a joyous reunion; but all I could think about was how this thing was going to play out. Later, Elvis had a giant hit with a song called, "It's Now or Never." I already knew the feeling.

CHAPTER TWENTY

It's Now or Never

Rex

My brother had no way of knowing how much inner turmoil I was experiencing. I wanted to tell him everything on the ride home, but I was too mentally, physically, and emotionally exhausted. Instead, I let him do all the talking.

Doyle brought me up-to-date on my family and friends while I sat back and listened. When we arrived home my mother took one look at me and knew something was amiss.

As if my emotional pin-balling wasn't taking enough of a toll, I was still hopped up on amphetamines and looked like I had run home behind the car. I hadn't slept soundly in days, had dark circles under my eyes, and was rail thin, tipping the scales at 140 pounds.

"Son, you look like death warmed over," my mother said, tears welling up in her eyes. "What is the matter, son?"

She made several attempts to find out what was wrong, but only ended up in tears. I did not want her or any of my family members to worry about me, so I said nothing. The first few days at home I spent sleeping and sulking, and not necessarily in that order.

Elisabeth was all I could think about. I was praying she would call. She meant everything to me. I desperately missed her and felt like I might explode with anxiety. This went on for five days. Then came my salvation, when late one evening the call I wanted more than anything in the whole world came. And the news it brought couldn't have been better.

"Rex, honey, I couldn't stop thinking about you," Elisabeth said. "I have good news. Elvis told me I was free to date whomever I please. Do you know anybody that might be interested?"

No drug has been invented that can cause the euphoria that I experienced right then. If one ever is, they'd better put it under hydrostatic-lock and throw away the key. I told Elisabeth I was coming for her, and without explaining the whole story to my family, I informed them that I was going back to Memphis to claim my future wife. I told them I had fallen in love with a beautiful German girl.

I was too excited to sleep that night, and stayed up making plans. As far as handling Elvis, I decided I would be humble and thank him for his generosity and friendship and then decline his kind job offer. I knew in my heart of hearts that I could never tolerate Elisabeth answering to Elvis at the snap of his fingers. If I worked for him too, I would have to witness this on a daily basis. I would have ended up in a room with padded walls and wearing a straitjacket.

Speaking of outfits, the following morning I went to the best men's clothing store in town. I bought myself some snazzy-looking threads using a good part of the money I had won in the craps game on the train. I wanted to look my best for the occasion. I borrowed my dad's 1957 Bel Air Chevrolet and hit the road for Memphis.

When I arrived at the front gate of Graceland, Uncle Vester immediately recognized me and gave me clearance to pull my car into the circular driveway near the front door. Vester informed Elvis that I was at the gate via the intercom system, and the man himself warmly greeted me at the front door.

"Rexadus, ol' boy, I knew you'd be back," Elvis said with a cocky laugh. Elvis' ego would never permit him to even think that anybody could walk away from the chance to live, work, and play at his side. The world was full of people who would have volunteered for that duty for the prestige of saying they were with Elvis.

I saw Elisabeth out of the corner of my eye as I greeted a group of Elvis' friends in the living room. I didn't make direct eye contact with Elisabeth for fear that Elvis would suspect something.

Was I nervous? Who wouldn't be? But at the same time, I had an inner calm, because I knew the objective that I was determined to achieve. This was "Operation Exodus Rexadus," and I had trained for it a long time. My military training included making practical choices and decisions, and then following through to the completion of the job. I felt confident I was going to win. It helped, too, that I had a strong sense of Divine Providence at work.

"Can we go somewhere and talk in private?" I asked Elvis quietly in front of the guys. Elvis immediately excused himself from the group and took me upstairs to his private bedroom. There I wasted no time getting to the point.

"Elvis, I've thought over your generous offer, but I've decided to go back to work for the same firm I was with before going into the Army," I told him, looking him right in the eye and speaking in measured tones. All primed for a war, I didn't even get a skirmish. Elvis didn't flinch, rant, rave, cajole, or come at me with inscrutable karate maneuvers. He just quietly said he understood and wished me the best of luck. I wondered if the Colonel had talked to him in the meantime. In any case, I had completed just half of my mission. I wasn't leaving Graceland until I could get Elisabeth out of there, too.

Pressing my advantage, I mentioned that I had a few days before I had to start my job.

"Stay as long as you want," Elvis graciously said. "Make yourself at home."

If this was a script, I couldn't have written it better myself. Elvis was in the midst of dressing for an evening at the movies with the gang. He had rented out an entire theater for an after-hours private showing, and was looking forward to enjoying himself. Elvis was looking into the big walled mirror at himself. I was directly behind him, helping him with his tuxedo suspenders. I figured I might as well go for the grand slam.

"Elvis, would you mind if I took Elisabeth out on a date tonight?" I asked in my most humble tone. This time he didn't answer right away. Clearly a nerve had been struck. He remained silent for the next minute, as I held my breath. Finally, the King issued his decree.

"Rexadus, you know Elisabeth will never love anybody but me," he said.

Now my nerves twitched. I had hit Elvis in the most vulnerable spot — his ego; and his visceral counterattack stung. But all of a sudden, Elvis switched gears.

"Heck, I'm glad you're taking her out," he smiled. "I know I can count on you to treat her like a lady." Home free! I almost sprinted for the door, and just as I had my hand on the doorknob, Elvis summoned me back.

"Hey Rexadus, I have a great idea. Why don't you and Elisabeth come with us to the theater?" Maybe I'd only hit a triple after all. Now I had to think fast before I got picked off the base.

"Thank you for the invitation, and I appreciate you thinking of us, but I have something else in mind for tonight," I answered. Elvis didn't look thrilled, but he let the matter go. I wanted to run through Graceland screaming and hollering like a 14-year-old who'd just accidentally run into Elvis Presley. But I forced myself to calmly walk down the stairs to find Elisabeth and personally deliver our Emancipation Proclamation.

"Honey," I said when I found her. "I am taking you to a drive-in movie tonight. Just you and me." She stood there in obvious shock, and I suggested that she probably ought to get ready before the master of the plantation had second thoughts. For the first time in months, I was at peace with myself.

I don't know what movie Elvis and the gang saw that night, and I couldn't tell you anything about the one that provided the background noise to Elisabeth's and my lovestruck reunion, either. We had a lot of lost time to make up for — along with some more planning to do. It was time for both of us to take our leave, once and for all, from Graceland. Preferably, without Elvis being any the wiser.

Were he to find out, we knew there would be a big scene. There always was when things didn't go according to Elvis' plan. We decided that tomorrow Elisabeth would have Janie Wilbanks pick her up at Graceland. Elisabeth had already phoned her parents in front of Elvis to let them know she was planning on a visit to their home in Hialeah, Florida. She'd tell Elvis that Janie was taking her to the airport.

She'd go to the airport, all right — but to meet me. Elisabeth wouldn't even tell Janie that part until they were on the way there.

I got Elisabeth back to Graceland at a decent hour. I knew Elvis and his gang would be watching movies until the wee hours of the morning. We snuck a kiss good night and went to our respective rooms to spend our final hours at Graceland in tense anticipation.

The next day, I let Elvis know that I had to leave for home in a few hours to start work sooner than I had expected. Elisabeth devised a story about spending the night with Janie before heading out to Miami the following day. Though we hated lying and plotting on the sly, we knew our plan would only work if we did it that way.

Before we left, Elisabeth and I both went to Grandma's room to bid her farewell. We couldn't deceive her. She meant too much to us, and we thought she would be thrilled with the results of the spadework she'd done in Germany. We wanted her blessing but what we got instead was excommunicated.

"Rex and Elisabeth, I urge you to confess your sins to Elvis," Grandma said desperately, as if she were confused that God and Elvis were one and the same. Then, as Grandma stormed out of her room and went downstairs to the kitchen, she mumbled that she didn't want to have anything further to do with us. Whoever said blood was thicker than water would have been right at home in Graceland.

Back downstairs, I shook hands with Lamar Fike, Cliff Gleaves, Red West, Sonny West (who I had just met for the first time that day), Billy Smith, George Klein, and Alan Fortas. Just then, Elvis asked me to help him with one last karate demonstration for old time's sake. It occurred to me that his real intention might be to literally kick me out the door; but I obliged and nothing untoward happened.

When it finally came time to break clean and for good, our farewell was oddly mechanical and emotionless. Elvis was sure I would be back, so it wasn't really final to him. I thanked him for all the wonderful times we shared and for opening his home to me in Germany, for the fun and games, and then we laughed about our adventures in Paris.

"Rexadus, come back and visit anytime, you're always welcome here," Elvis said. He sounded totally sincere, and I was grateful. And also a bit guilty. Apparently everybody else at Graceland sensed something was going on between Elisabeth and me. Elvis seemed to be the only one in the dark, and he had given us permission to date each other. So why were we so afraid? One reason was that we both knew we could never tell him the truth without a huge confrontation. I even feared it could get physical between Elvis and me, and I certainly did not want Elisabeth to witness something like that. We just didn't want to deal with his wrath, nor with the embarrassment and guilt trip he would have heaped on us in front of the others — something we had seen him do to people many times in the past. Most important, we could not betray the people that knew and kept our secret. If Elvis found out from us about our romance, and then discovered his friends and family knew about it and never told him, there would be serious repercussions all around.

Lamar and Cliff knew for sure what Elisabeth and I had in mind, and they didn't tip off the boss, although it's possible they tipped off the guys. I think in some way they and the rest felt that Elvis deserved this. Maybe they were rooting for me because I had the guts to take one of Elvis' girls right from under his nose. I suppose Grandma didn't dare tell Elvis for fear he would find out she was actually the one who played Cupid to us.

I gave Elisabeth a quick kiss goodbye and she reassured me everything would go as planned. "Don't worry, Rex, we have made it this far. I will see you in about 30 minutes. Then we will be with each other forever," she said.

On my way out, I went through the kitchen for one last try with Grandma. I sincerely wanted to thank her for all she had done for Elisabeth and me. Various staff were around and I could see Grandma was upset as she saw me approaching. As I got closer she began backing away from me as if I was morphing into something hideous — Frau Pieper? — right in front of her eyes.

"Get out of here, you snake!" she hissed at me. That was a stunner, and I didn't try to reason with her. I was hurt, of course, but understood that she must have felt all bonds of friendship between us had to be cut for the sake of her relationship with Elvis. Or maybe Grandma was upset because Elisabeth was like a daughter to her and I was taking her away.

When I left Graceland, I knew I would never be welcome there again by any member of the Presley family. On the drive to the airport my mind drifted over my friendship with Elvis. I was ending a fascinating chapter of my life as his friend, sometime protector, and confidante. For two years I had been one of his closest buddies. I was there to comfort him after his mother's death. I pulled guard duty for him on many occasions. We played pool together, studied karate, and even sang together. Spending time with Elvis allowed me to see and do things most people only dreamt about. Most importantly, through my involvement with Elvis, I met my soulmate.

Thinking of Elisabeth brought me back to the present, and I wondered how her escape was going. Not without a hitch, I later found out. Just as Elisabeth and Janie reached the front gate to leave Graceland, Elisabeth realized she had forgotten to pick up her last paycheck. They turned around and drove back up the circular driveway, stopping at the front steps. Elvis came running out of the house with Elisabeth's check in hand.

As he reached the car and offered the check, he looked Elisabeth square in the eye and delivered a bombshell. "Are you going to meet Rex?" he asked. Busted on the verge of a clean getaway! Her heart hammering inside her chest, Elisabeth could feel the blood rushing to her face. According to Lamar's version of events, delivered years later, apparently Cliff had told Elvis all about us within moments of Elisabeth's departure.

You couldn't be around show business types without become a pretty good performer yourself. "No," Elisabeth told him — and Elvis bought it. Maybe his ego just wouldn't let him believe she was choosing me over him. He handed over the check and waved them off.

Meanwhile, I was waiting at the Memphis Airport. During my own drive there from Graceland, I had timed the distance. Elisabeth and Janie should have been at the airport 15 to 20 minutes after me, but with Elisabeth having to go back for her paycheck, and the close call at Graceland's front door, it was 40 minutes before they finally arrived. I was going crazy wondering what happened, and as I paced the driveway in front of the airport all kinds of wild scenarios presented themselves.

Maybe Elisabeth got caught, somebody told Elvis, or perhaps Elisabeth got cold feet and changed her mind at the last minute. My insecurities kicked into high gear. How could I think a beautiful girl like Elisabeth would really leave Elvis for me? Who was I kidding anyway?

The King and Ann-Margret never played a love scene like the one that unfolded after Janie's car pulled up. When Elisabeth got out of the car, she made a mad dash into my arms. All I could do was hold her tightly and kiss her.

"I am so glad to see you, sweetheart, you are the best thing that ever happened to me," I managed to get out the moment we came up for air. "I love you with all of my heart."

"I love you too, honey," wheezed my girl, "and I want to spend every second of the rest of my life with you."

When we finally unclinched, we explained everything to Janie, who said she was leaving so the "lovebirds could be alone." We thanked her for everything and hugged her goodbye. Finally it was just the two of us (unless you counted the folks coming in and out of the airport). We were finally free to love one another without having to look over our shoulder.

I had selected a hotel near the airport for us to spend the next 24 hours alone. Then Elisabeth would fly out to Miami to visit her parents the next day. In a couple of days, Lamar was scheduled to deliver the yellow Lincoln Elvis had given her. Elvis told Elisabeth he would continue paying her salary and that she could come back whenever she was ready to resume her job as his private secretary.

The next afternoon, I drove Elisabeth back to the airport. We kissed and hugged until I was cut off at the gate. She had a window seat on the plane and we waved to each other until it pulled away.

Once Elisabeth left Graceland for me, there was no need for me to formally propose. We both knew we were going to get married. It wasn't a question of if, but when. She left Elvis Presley, the King of Rock and Roll, for me, and it wasn't merely to become my girlfriend.

I walked her down the aisle when we first met at the German movie house. On June 4, 1960, I did it again to make Elisabeth Claudia Stefaniak my wife. It was a simple ceremony in a little white Catholic Church in Union City, Tennessee, about 15 miles from Dresden. Only immediate family and close friends were in attendance.

We had sent Elvis a telegram inviting him to our wedding, but he did not respond. We expected Elvis would be upset when he received the news, but we hoped that maybe deep down inside he would understand. I suppose the telegram was at least a little bit intended to rub his nose in the fact that I had beaten him to win the affection of such a beautiful and wonderful woman. I had an ego, too.

The following Christmas, Elisabeth received an autographed 8 x 10 photograph of Elvis. There was no note or message, just the picture and the signature. Maybe Elvis was letting her know what she had passed up. That was the last we ever heard from him.

A couple months before our first wedding anniversary, Elisabeth sent Grandma a card. Maybe Grandma still took a reptilian view of us, but we wanted her to know the feeling wasn't mutual and that we would always love her. It was a pleasant surprise to receive a letter back from her dated April 11, 1961. It read:

Dear Elisabeth,

I was so glad to hear from you both! I would love to see you. Dee and Vernon said to tell you hello. The weather here is very pretty today; it has been raining for the past month. How is Rex? Elvis is in Honolulu now making another movie and won't be back until June.

Well I must go — I'm not feeling too well today. Please write again soon — I love hearing from you both. I love you Elisabeth and always will. Be sure to answer my letter now.

Love Grandma

Her response led us to believe we finally had her forgiveness. However, there was still one person whose forgiveness still eluded us.

Epilogue

We sat down several times between 1960 and Elvis' death in 1977 and tried to write him a letter of explanation. Somehow, we were never able to do it. We wanted to explain to Elvis why we did what we did, and apologize for how we did it. We were immature and afraid of confrontation.

Many people have wondered why we did not have any further contact with Elvis after our marriage. The main reason, I suppose, is that I was still jealous of his name being mentioned by Elisabeth in my presence.

It took a good decade for me to get over the hurt of remembering Elvis' and Elisabeth's relationship, but as our marriage became stronger, so did my self-esteem. By the time Elvis made his famous comeback in 1969, we were both genuinely happy for his renewed success, and any hard feelings I had for him had been exorcised.

From 1960 to 1976, Elisabeth and I lived in Charlotte, North Carolina, where I became Baker Equipment & Engineering's vice-president over their Southern Division's four branches.

It was while we were living there that we had one last opportunity to see Elvis again. He was scheduled to make an appearance at the Charlotte Coliseum on April 13, 1972. Lamar Fike came to visit us and we asked him if he thought it would be a good idea to try to reconnect with Elvis. Lamar had always been straight with us, and he didn't whitewash his feelings now.

"Don't do it," he said. "He will embarrass you in front of the others. You don't need him, you've got a good life. Don't give him the opportunity to screw it up by getting another hold on you."

Elvis and Priscilla had eventually married, had a baby, but now they were splitting. Lamar said Elvis' behavior was more erratic than ever, what with that and the fact that he was heavily medicating himself. The combination, he said, made Elvis increasingly difficult to deal with. We accepted Lamar's advice, and never tried to see or contact Elvis.

Most people of our generation can recall where they were and what they were doing on August 16, 1977. Elisabeth and I were living in West Germany when we heard the news on the radio about Elvis' tragic death. I honestly can't say we were very shocked, having seen his most recent photos and knowing about Elvis' unrestrained lifestyle. But we were very saddened and sorry that such a great talent had gone by the wayside. Elvis had been our friend and our benefactor. We wouldn't have traded our time with him for anything, but we chose to make our own life with each other and we know it was the right choice.

We've had several decades to think about our relationship with Elvis Presley and what made him such a complex human being, and his life such a contradiction.

To start with, Elvis was raised in utter poverty — the son of a Mississippi sharecropper — and he had very few material things. Elvis was 10 years old when World War II ended. Economically, our country was in rebuilding mode, and everything was on ration. Elvis' parents went through the Great Depression of the

1930s, which left a mark on almost everybody in the United States. Elvis grew up poor and then, suddenly, almost overnight, became very rich and famous.

Following World War II, the greatest and longest economic boom in world history was launched, and the great American dream came true for Elvis — a boy from the cotton farmland of Mississippi. His music fit the times perfectly. He was the ideal representative to present rock and roll music to the world. With the help of Colonel Tom Parker, who was the perfect manager for him, they scaled the dizzying heights of superstardom.

It would not be easy for any human being to handle that much sudden fame and fortune. It may come as a surprise to know that Elvis was even more amazed than anyone else about his incredible off-the-charts success.

Elvis was kind of like the Shah of Iran was during his prime. They both demanded and required that everybody around them exhibit unconditional loyalty. Elvis was jealous of any independent relationship, male or female, forged by people around him. He wanted his friends' and employees' undivided attention and devotion. His relationship with you came before anything else. You literally belonged to him, and did exactly what he wanted when he wanted it.

Elvis was insecure and unsure of himself, which is why I think he gravitated to prescription medicine, and ultimately abused it. He needed lots of people around him to constantly admire him and tell him how great he was. Perhaps this came from the constant doting of his mother.

If Elvis wanted something of yours, he took it. He was jealous of anybody that could make him feel insecure. You had to be very careful what was said around Elvis because he could turn on you in a second. Elvis was suspicious of everybody, and yet his ego caused him to be naive in many situations.

Of course, Elvis could never believe that any of his women could ever fall in love with another man. Even so, he was afraid enough of that prospect that he would constantly remind those around him not to have personal relationships with each other, and anyone caught doing so would be kicked out instantly. These negative traits were all a direct result of Elvis' emotional immaturity and instant fame. Anybody could be affected in the same manner by such circumstances.

Elvis' good traits far outnumbered the bad. He was sincere, personable, kind-hearted, humorous, and was a lot of fun to be with. But perhaps his greatest gift was his special way of making everyone feel he was the most important person in the world to him. His personality was magnetic, and it was magical to be with him. When he looked at you, it felt like he was looking right into your soul.

Elvis was extremely kind-hearted and didn't give a second thought about buying someone — even complete strangers — books, clothes, jewelry, or expensive cars. Of course, it depended on his mood.

He was honorable, especially toward his mother and father. He always saw to it that his family was well provided for. There were times in Germany when Vernon was involved with other women which made it difficult for Elvis. But not once did he ever dishonor his father.

Elvis also had a great sense of humor. He could always find something funny about every situation, and many times this would get him into trouble when he was supposed to be serious. But he got away with it, I think because he could charm the pants off people with his "yes ma'ams" and "no ma'ams." Elvis was always extremely well-mannered in the public eye.

There will never be another man like Elvis. He was destined for greatness. I think God had a plan for Elvis. There is no telling what great influence Elvis could have had on future generations had he chosen a different road. But this matter is not for me or anyone else to judge.

Elisabeth and I have often wondered — if we had the time with Elvis to do over again, would or could we have done anything differently? Our answer always comes back "no" because we don't believe anything else could have been done without changing the ultimate outcome for the worst. We believe without a doubt that Elvis would not have approved of our marriage had we told him about our secret dates. A half-truth in this case would have been worse than none at all. His pride and ego would have precluded a solution agreeable to all, and a lot of unnecessary problems would have followed.

We have been happily married now for over four decades, celebrating our 48th anniversary on June 4, 2008. I have done fairly well in the business world, holding one position in 1975 as corporate vice-president of operations for Baker Equipment Company with over 250 employees and seven branches up and down the Eastern seaboard of the United States.

Elisabeth became a wonderful homemaker and helpmate, encouraging me every step of the way and being the anchor in our relationship. She is the epitome of the old saying, "Behind every successful man is a great woman."

In 1966, we adopted our son, Donald Rex Mansfield, Jr., who has been a constant source of joy and excitement.

Ten years later, I met the Lord Jesus Christ as my personal

Savior, and He has transformed my life. My wife and son have also become "born-again" Christians. We are a Christian family and God has met all our needs (abundantly) according to His glorious riches in Christ Jesus. Before Christ we had more materialistic and ego-centered goals in our lives, thinking these would make us happy. As a Christian family, knowing that we are now in God's will, we have a peace inside us that surpasses all human understanding.

Later in 1976, I took a job in international sales for a Texas firm who sent the family to Europe in early 1977 for two and a half years. Living in Europe was a great experience as we learned more about the world that God created for his children. We lived in Texas from 1979 to 1987, where I worked in export sales for the same firm.

In 1987, my career took us back to Europe again. A decade later, we found ourselves back in the States as a semi-retired couple enjoying life to the fullest. We love to go for drives in the Great Smoky Mountains, visiting the numerous attractions, going to live theatre shows and eating out at some of the hundreds of restaurants in the area where we live. Also, we love playing with and loving our little dog, Buddy, who is a mix of Fox Terrier and Jack Russell.

God has recently given me a new job consulting for Mr. Joseph G. "Skip" Baker, Jr., the grandson of the firm I began working for in 1960. We are doing the same work we did four decades ago, but with a new goal of ministering to businesses through corporate chaplains of America.

How do we feel about Elvis today? We think he was the greatest entertainer the world has ever known. Given Elvis' divine musical talent, it is no wonder that his popularity is ever-growing. Hearing an Elvis song reminds us of the talented man we once knew, and how thankful we are to him for bringing us together. We are especially fond of his gospel recordings. Our favorite ones are: "You'll Never Walk Alone," "I Believe," "Where No One Stands Alone," "Precious Lord," "Without Him," and "He Touched Me." I recall Elvis singing them at the house in Germany, and many times I joined in.

Today my biggest regret is that with my new Christian faith, perhaps we could have somehow influenced Elvis. If we could have seen him prior to his death, we could have shared how Christ changed our lives. Now we can only hope and pray that Elvis is with God, and, that he can now understand and forgive us.

That his soul may rest in peace with God is our constant hope.

Rex and Elisabeth Mansfield in 2005